HAPPINESS IS AN IMAGINARY LINE IN THE SAND

HAPPINESS IS AN IMAGINARY LINE IN THE SAND

THOMAS LLOYD QUALLS

WAYFARER BOOKS
WWW.WAYFARERBOOKS.ORG

© 2021, 2024 text by Thomas Lloyd Qualls

Wayfarer Books supports copyright. Copyright fuels creativity, encourages diverse voices, promotes free speech, and creates a vibrant culture. Thank you for buying an authorized edition of this book and for complying with copyright laws by not reproducing, scanning, or distributing any part of it in any form without permission. You are supporting writers and allowing us to continue to publish books for every reader.

All Rights Reserved
Published in 2021 by Homebound Publications
Published in 2024 by Wayfarer Books
Cover Design and Interior Design by Connor Wolfe
978-1953340245 First Edition Trade Paperback
979-8-9910415-5-3 Second Edition Paperback

10 9 8 7 6 5 4 3 2

Wayfarer Books is committed to ecological stewardship.
We greatly value the natural environment and invest in conservation.

PO Box 1601, Northampton, MA 01060

wayfarer@homeboundpublications.com

HOMEBOUNDPUBLICATIONS.COM & WAYFARERBOOKS.ORG

CONTENT

I. BEGINNINGS & OTHER POINTS ON THE CIRCLE

    1. Each Day Asks This   3
    2. Begin   7
    3. Where to Start   11
    4. Start Over   15
    5. Keep Finding Your Center   19
    6. Stay Curious   23

II. LOST & FOUND

    7. There Are Days   29
    8. Grapple   33
    9. Benefit of the Doubt   37
    10. Finding Beauty in Darkness   41
    11. The Unknowable World   47
    12. Lessons From My Son   51

III. NEW WORLD & OLD RUBBLE

    13. Building the New World   59
    14. Open   63
    15. Trust   67
    16. Dig Deeper   71
    17. The Hidden World   75
    18. How to Blend the Worlds   79

IV. WORDS & THEIR NOTICEABLE ABSENCE

19. The Ingredients of Words	85
20. Elevate the Word	89
21. Let's Talk About Writing	93
22. You're Not the Boss of Me	97
23. Someday Words	101
24. Walking Lessons	105

V. ART & THE SEARCH FOR BEAUTY

25. Your Job is to Find Beauty	111
26. Save the World, Buy Art	115
27. Believe in Art	119
28. Storied Life	123
29. Notes on Madness & Art	127
30. Create It	129

VI. LOVE & OTHER MISADVENTURES

31. Love	137
32. What is Love?	141
33. Lonely Hearts Club	145
34. The Heart of Ewe	149
35. WTAF	151
36. More Than This	155

VII. LONGING & BELONGING

37. You Belong Here	161
38. Give It Up	165
39. We're All Outsiders	169
40. The Things We Want	173
41. Follow Me	177
42. Howl	181

VIII. TIME & SPACE

43. A Space Between the Notes	189
44. Roiling In Dough	191
45. Be Free	195
46. A Void Is Not Something You Fill	203
47. Enough	207
48. How to Navigate an Inversion	211

IX. INVITATIONS & PERMISSION SLIPS

49. Fight Back	217
50. Go Ahead	221
51. Be Brave	225
52. Unravel	229
53. Be That	233
54. Thrive	237

X. DREAM MONSTERS & AWAKENINGS

55. Feelings Are Like Cats	243
56. Be Kind	249
57. Lighten Up	253
58. What Are You Laughing At?	257
59. The Shifting World	261
60. Don't Stop	265

XI. TRANSFORMATIONS & ACCIDENTAL DISCOVERIES

61. Splintered Oneness	271
62. Life Would Like Your Full Attention	275
63. The Art of Holding Hands	281
64. The Earth is an Enlightened Master	285
65. Feather in the Wind	289
66. Happiness is An Imaginary Line in the Sand	293

Bibliography
Acknowledgements
About the Author
About the Press

I

BEGINNINGS
& Other Points on the Circle

1

EACH DAY ASKS THIS

Each day asks this of us. That we forget the one before.

Each day asks this of us. That we not hold too tightly to the sight of flowers that bloom so unexpectedly all over our yards, our streets, our city. To the daubs of joy that suddenly saturate our awareness of just how lonely we've been for color all the long gray winter. That we allow these things to come and to go in their time. That we not grieve as the once vibrant petals wither and fall, scattering and collecting, unceremoniously, in the fence corners and the gutters.

That we love and let go of beauty.

Each day asks this of us. That we forget our endless disappointments, our not-so-quiet rage. That we hit whatever reset is required. That we turn and face it, put on our makeup, polish our shoes. That we grind the coffee and adorn the oatmeal. That we approach uncertainty unflinchingly, unjaded. That we turn yesterday's cheek, unclinch our fists, offer an open palm.

That we believe in it. As if it had never, ever let us down.

Each day asks this of us. That we rediscover ourselves. That we forget everything we knew about yesterday. That we wake up in the same bed, eat the same food, put on the same clothes, look at the same mirror, and see these all as brand new. That we wash our faces and change our socks, always asking who these things belong to.

Each day asks this of us. That we remember our cells are reimagining themselves faster than we can change our minds. That everything, absolutely everything in our universe is on its way to somewhere else, something else. That it is not possible to stand still.

Though we sit on pillows and strive to quiet our minds. Though we simplify and simplify and simplify. Though we journey to the desert. Though we strip down to nakedness. Each day asks this of us and more.

Each day asks this of us. That we look the same way upon the flowers and the snow, the clouds and the sun. That we enjoy all the things that are there and not long for what is not. That we love the heat of midday as we do the sunrise and sunset. That the dark sky hold as much sway as the full moon.

That we understand spring's parade of pinks and whites and yellows will be gone by the time these words are read. That we not mourn the clean comfort of snow-covered mountains as their luminosity fades to earth and rock. That we abide the rolling coastal sheep grounds, as they surrender their lush carpets to the summer sun. That we accept that the vibrant immediacy of redeeming passion that rises to meet our deepest desires will also slip from memory's grasp. That we forgive the fact that all this and more will disappear.

Each day asks this of us. That we open our hands. That we let go of what we are clinging to, to make room for the new gifts it has for us.

That we accept that there is nothing to lose and nothing to gain. That there is only what this day has brought to us. That there is no hoarding, no saving, no burying in the yard. That there is not more in the back. That regardless of what we are told, there is always enough to share.

Each day asks this of us. That we put salve on our bruises and sew up our heartbreaks. That we record the victories and put the trophies on the shelf. That we clean and oil the chain, put new air in the tires. That we put in a fresh ribbon and stack clean sheets.

That we be willing to entertain the idea that disappointment and desire deserve unfamiliar names.

Each day asks this of us. That we show up. And nothing more. No hiding beneath the covers. No resting on laurels. No reaching for back issues. No sitting on the bench. No calling in sick. No need to save the world.

That against great odds we must make ourselves understand that we cannot find love by tracking its scent. That the bra she left in your bed, the scent of his shirt, our dog-eared diaries, the photo stream in the cloud—each of the things that are too precious to name—we must somehow comprehend that we found them because we were there at the time. Not because we were looking for yesterday.

Each day asks this of us. That we live it. That we breathe

while there is air to float upon. That we move while there is earth to hold us. That we not grieve our too crooked paths. And that we not shirk from the beauty of being.

2

BEGIN

Whatever it is, Goethe says, begin it.

AT LEAST, that's what some people say he said. The Buddha speaks about the beginner's mind. Jesus teaches that the Kingdom of Heaven belongs to children. Meister Eckhart tells us to trust the magic of beginnings. And a new year often brings us to a similar state of mind.

Maybe that's what we're all after with those promises to stop doing any number of the self-sabotaging things we've been doing and finally stick to something we say we will or won't do. But what I want to talk about goes beyond such temporary solutions. What I'm talking about is more of a fundamental realignment of awareness.

For us to truly understand the power of beginnings is for us to wake up every day in a new world. We must embrace beginner's mind, question all our questions, give away all our answers, stand naked in the sunrise, and truly believe in starting over. To begin is to believe down deep in your indestructible soil that transformative change is possible. Right now.

More than this, to begin is to live in the most immediate right now you can imagine. That all your yesterdays only matter in that they were the vehicle to bring you to this right now, fully enveloping, beautifully poignant, present moment of beginning.

A beginning is stealthy.

In *Dune*, Princess Irulan reminds us that, "A beginning is a very delicate time." Which is true, in the sense of the fragility of an idea or an action or a thought that has not yet rooted, not sprouted buds, not caught on. Another way to look at it is that beginnings are easy. Because mostly, nobody notices them. They've not suffered from overexposure, embarrassment, partial failure, the need to reboot.

Beginnings often slip through the cracks, down onto the floor, past the ticket-takers, and right up to the stage, before anyone is the wiser. Nobody notices until they are way past the beginning, until there's enough momentum to survive scrutiny.

And then, it's kind of too late. Not too late, as in too late to begin. Too late as in there's no undoing a beginning that nobody saw coming, that's already in the middle of being, that's half way through its own realization. Just let her finish what she was saying.

The beginning is enticing.

The beginning is enticing because everything is new and exhilarating, like a first kiss. And it is different than just being in the now. In the beginning, things are always beautiful. Sure, we are present, we are aware, but we are also breathtakingly alive.

There is an eagerness, an anticipation, and also an overwhelming sense of right now. It is not merely a hope for things to come, it is an embodiment of the desire to stand right where we are, to soak it up. To be wide awake. To not care about tomorrow, because right now, we are turned on. This brand new [anything and everything we are fully enmeshed with in the beginning] has reminded us of the beauty of being fully awake.

The newness of anything is seductive. A new car, a new house, a new lover, a new town, a new restaurant, a new flower in the yard. But the beginning takes us beyond the surface sexiness of such things and into a parallel realm where we not only are awakened to the saturation of beauty all around us, but confident in our newfound ability to access it, to create more.

A beginning marks a point that lights up the circle.

I've said before there are no beginnings and no endings, only random points on a circle, staccato notes on a page. That our stories are woven like snakes around a divining rod. Not stretched out and laid flat.

If the story is circular, then why does a beginning matter? For the same reason that staccato notes matter. Because the beginning is a flash of light, illuminating everything in its path, waking us up, giving us a glimpse of the whole.

So if you are tired of trying to be present in your life but find yourself not there most of the time, considering entering a world where everything is always new. In the words of Michael Stipe, *begin the begin.*

3

WHERE TO START

So there's been another mass shooting. And another. And another. A bunch of old white men voted to defund Planned Parenthood and deprive basic healthcare for millions of women. Several multinational corporations tucked away more billions of dollars offshore, refusing to pay taxes, and putting at risk all the public systems so necessary to each of us.

Everywhere we look things seem unsustainable, upside down, and broken beyond repair. Things like climate change, health care, and religious wars, or Wall Street, Monsanto, and the amount of time we spend on Facebook. People everywhere continue to fear and hate other people, cultures, beliefs, or really anything they don't understand.

Meanwhile, the majority of us are just trying to make rent and remember our passwords.

Most of us want to believe in a better world. We want to believe it is possible to find happiness. To live peaceful lives. To laugh easily and more often. We want to believe that self-empowerment is possible. That all the quotes from the spiritual masters are true. That the lives we imagine for ourselves are real and possible. And that we can build a better world.

We want to make good on our resolutions to meditate regularly, to do more yoga, and to spend more time giving back to our communities. We want to be better citizens of the world. Or, maybe we'd just like to make it through the day without yelling. Whatever our goals, we want to empower ourselves to make real and lasting changes, and to inspire others to do the same. Whatever our ideals, we really want to figure out a way to help make the world a better place to live.

But we haven't got the slightest idea where to start.

Like looking at a tangle of Christmas lights the size of a beach ball, without any visible beginning or end. Or staring into an open box of 5,000 puzzle pieces depicting Dalmatians in a snow storm. It all seems insurmountable. Beyond our reach. Above our pay grades.

And then there's this voice in our heads that keeps whispering that all our hopes for a better world are born of fairy tales. That the real world is nothing like the world we imagine. That it is time to grow up and accept that life is little more than struggle and heartbreak. And after a while, we start to listen. And we start to believe that the voice is right.

Relax. At best the voice is only half right.

If we are paying attention, we probably know the world is light and dark. Possibly exactly half of each. But I don't know if there's any way to measure this. And like your cereal box, it might be based upon weight, not volume. The thing is, whichever one we're looking at usually happens to eclipse a realistic view of the other. And so we end up with a skewed perspective of what is real.

Yes, the world is a messy place, filled with all variant gradations of gray. Which somehow makes it harder and easier to navigate. What is important in starting to fix the world is acknowledging that maybe it doesn't need fixing.

What do you mean *doesn't need fixing?*

What I mean is, it could be that the world is as Anaïs Nin reminded us it was, when she said, *We do not see things as they are, we see them as we are.* Or it could be like Robert Pirsig's explanation that, *We take a handful of sand from the endless landscape of awareness around us and call that handful of sand the world.* So maybe it isn't the world that needs fixing, but our view of it.

Or maybe it really is that broken. And maybe we just need to let the old world die. Let it crumble and fall at our feet. And we build a new one in its place. Brick by brick. Word by word. Breath by breath. But still there is the question of where to start?

We can start by acknowledging the light.

By standing in its glow as much as possible. By letting it illuminate us and our paths. By tending to our own sparks, feeding them, and keeping them burning. Then we can look around us at the fires of others. We can notice when theirs have gone out. Because, let's be honest, that happens to all of us. But with just a touch of our light, we can bring their fires back to life.

So we pass the torch. And we light and relight. And we understand there are such things as rain and wind and green wood. And so we stay awake and keep watch over each other's fires.

And we also acknowledge the dark.

Because we need it, too. Because otherwise there would be nothing but surgery lights. And who could live like that? Not me. I wear sunglasses when it's cloudy outside. I'm not saying we need to embrace acts of violence. But we need to understand and accept that rage and confusion live inside each of us.

And I'm not saying to wallow in despair, but to acknowledge that there is beauty in the dark. And that the darkness and the light need one another. And because without their tension, there would be no story. Without clouds all the colors wash away.

And then what?

We believe. That's what. And we act on our beliefs. And we keep imagining what the new world can look like. And we keep building it.

Dream by dream. Word by word. Breath by breath. Spark by spark.

Because this is how we make something real. Not by despairing or complaining or protesting. But by imagining. And by putting pen to paper. Words to voice. Hands to clay.

4

START OVER

We must be willing to let go of the life we planned
so as to have the life that is waiting for us.
—Joseph Campbell

WE LOVE A NEW YEAR. And not just because of the outrageous parties, the glitter, champagne, and black dresses. Not just the countdown and the kisses at midnight. Not even the day off, with parades, friends, and football.

Not that we don't love all those things. But mostly we love it because it's the one giant reset button that comes with our calendars every year. An excuse, not just to reuse or recycle, but to reboot. To start over. Whatever that means to you.

You could, if you wanted, flush everything that came before. Maybe your relationship reached the end of its natural life. Or it's the job, the tired car, yesterday's shoes, the outgrown apartment, or even your town that you need to kick to the curb.

For most of us, it's probably a little less dramatic. It could be just one or two little things. Like this painting I did last year. I love most of it, but there's this one part. Despite the need for all art to find its finishing place, I've got to fix this one. And a new year gives me permission to take it down from the wall and do that.

Whether it's big or small, can't we do this on any given day of the year, reboot our lives? Of course. Will we? Likely not. But January 01 stands before us on the horizon as the poster-child for the perennial possibility of second, third, and twenty-seventh chances.

Though, that's not the whole story. Part of us doesn't really want to start over. As much as we talk tough. Because, well, we've kind of grown attached to our dysfunction. We've been living our stories of why certain things don't work for us since before we can remember, and truthfully, we're just too damn lazy to tear up the manuscript and start over.

Take it from a writer, sometimes you've got to burn those pages. As enmeshed as you are with the story, the characters, and the script; as badly as you want to breathe life back into that anemic storyline, sometimes you've just got to take Faulkner's advice and kill your darlings. No matter how many re-writes you've been through trying to suture the wounds.

When I wrote the first draft of the novel *Waking Up at Rembrandt's*, it was about twice as long and had twice as many storylines. Then I put it aside for a little while. When I picked it up to read it with fresh eyes, I kind of hated it. But, like the worn-out stories we live for too long, I was reluctant to let it go.

One morning, pre-dawn, I sat down to write without any goal in mind. In that space, a new voice started flooding the pages. I couldn't channel the words fast enough. And some of them were lost to the ether. But it was the push I needed to pick up the novel again. And to tear it to shreds. The result was a new narrator, a new point of view, and a piece of art that was distilled down to its essence, with half as many characters and storylines. And this time, I didn't want to throw it away when I was done.

But it never would've happened if I hadn't been willing to start over. We've all got to let go of yesterday, in order to live today. We hear this, and we know it's true. And it is still harder than hard to actually do it.

Tomorrow, we say. We have time; we lie to ourselves. Because no one has time. Time cannot be had. All we really have is right now. And the giant red reset button that's available for the pushing every day of the year, no matter what the calendar tells us.

Whatever it is that isn't working in your life, change it. As has been said and said and said, this isn't a dress rehearsal. The remarkable thing is that we hear this, and we tell ourselves we understand it, yet we go right back to living the same story. We go right back to complaining about the same things. We go right back to the novel written in the wrong voice, the painting that just doesn't work, the same tired arguments with ourselves and others.

When what we need to do is to just stop. Press the button. Start over. No matter what you might think now. No matter what others may trick you into believing. Life is short. Quite unbelievably short, really. You, me, and everyone we know will wake up one day and be really pissed at our current selves for not hitting that button. And for not hitting it more often. Go ahead. No matter what the calendar says, hit that button.

5

KEEP FINDING YOUR CENTER

There are days when the coffee does not clear our heads, when pretty words cannot soothe our hearts. When our legs are unsteady, our feet untrustworthy, our next breath uncertain.

Life, it seems, does not come with any guarantees of fairness. There is no contract with the planet, the universe, or your higher power that mandates things go according to your design.

All our collective best hopes, our ideal notions of the way life ought to look, how things ought to be, these things have been getting smashed daily along with our faith in the human race. Still somehow we continue to believe in what is right, decent, just. Until little by little, one at a time, we don't.

I see you. I hear your words. I feel your silence. I understand your rage. And I ask myself what we can do on these days when we need something solid to keep us upright. What do we do when we've lost sight of the horizon and the stars, when we need some new tools to chart our course?

If you follow me, you know I don't pretend to have all the answers. (Most days I can barely articulate the questions.) But

I do know this much: The peace of mind we seek, the sense of hope, the path out of the fog, those things do not lie ahead of us in some imagined better future, but right here, in this present moment.

Like me, you are probably tired of hearing about the importance of being present, when you are not really even sure what the hell that means. So let me try to serve it up in a more palatable dish.

Here's the difficult truth: There is no such thing as tomorrow. For real. The future is imaginary. It is a projection of our minds. When tomorrow arrives, it isn't really tomorrow, but today. And the thing is, it hasn't really arrived from some distant land. It is simply the ongoing right now.

Now I don't understand how it is exactly that time is an illusion. Except that the masters assure us it is. They tell us that this linear idea of time—the one that almost every last one of us believes in, this image of one second following the next until something like 86,000 of them equal a day—this is really just a human construct we have designed to keep our brains from exploding with the information of how the universe actually works.

I know, this sounds like crazy hippy shit. But I'm pretty sure it's not. At least it isn't crazy. And if you stop for just a moment and just let yourself breathe, I think you'll find it to be true. Once you start to do this on a regular basis, you may agree with the masters that the only way to accomplish anything, including change, is to locate yourself in the present moment. To find your center and figure out how to stay there, how to operate there, and when you get thrown off, to return there. Again and again.

This is also what it takes to write. You have to lose yourself to the outside world, to your notion of time, to your expectations for the future, and just fall into the page. This might be why many of the ancient masters were also poets. This also why the great master painters made art that is timeless, that is still alive when we look at it today, even though it was painted decades or centuries ago.

Plato may have advocated for philosopher kings, but what we really need are poet kings. Artists. People who walk among us, eat and drink with us, yet see beyond the headlines. To figure out how to locate and keep your center, you must understand:

Time begs no forgivenesses,
gives no excuses,
won't be broken.
Though the mystics tell me
it bends.*

The world is bigger than our ideas of it. We must remember that. We must remember that no matter how unfair, surreal, or heartbreaking our world appears to become, these images are only one part of the story. One chapter, one version, one scene, one sketch, one soon-to-be-discarded draft. We must breathe through it.

Holding on to anger and resentment only makes those feelings hang around longer. Let them go. Exhale and make room for the new world.

6

STAY CURIOUS

Study hard what interests you the most in the most undisciplined, irreverent and original manner possible.
—Richard Feynman

IN OTHER WORDS, be like a child again. Not child*ish*, as almost all adults can be —which is far more annoying than it is endearing—but child*like*. A child is endlessly curious. Though a child does not really need to know the answers. A child just needs to question, to investigate, to dig, to root, and to turn over stones. Then to keep on digging, building, adding, and tearing down. And starting over with new questions and ideas.

The finding of things is fun, too. But it is not the most essential thing. The discovery of anything will do. Children are masters of serendipity. Their innate impulse is to question, and to go about looking for new things, whether they are water bugs or woozles. The important thing is the adventure, which really never ends. And which is only occasionally interrupted by the silliness of adults making them stop to eat, or to brush their teeth and put on jammies.

For children, the world is stuffed full of magic things. This is because, well, the world is actually stuffed full of magic things. Our prejudices are learned. We are not born with our narrow approaches to life and its inhabitants. Our natural inclination is to seek out and to celebrate the magic. Every day, all day long. I think this is why children annoy some adults and delight others. The annoyed ones don't want to be reminded of all that they've left behind. The delighted ones either still carry a healthy dose of magic with them, or they at least know where to find it.

Certainty is an illusion.

If there is evil in the world, which is at least debatable, the root of it most certainly lies in the desire for certainty. The older we get the more we realize how few absolutes there are in the world. But one of the absolutes we're all pretty sure about is change. Everything is on its way to somewhere else all the time. There is no standing still. There are no forever answers.

And so how could there really be certainty about anything. When we are young, we think that the answer to the question of who we are is answerable. If we are really precocious, we may even think we know who we are. Or maybe we think, it'll just take a little more examination, a little more life experience. The older we get, the more we understand that there could never be an answer to this question. And even if there were, it would be outdated as soon as we uttered it. In fact, we can't even answer the question of what we mean by the word "me."

As I've said before, it's okay to be uncertain. In fact, it is preferred. Imagine a world without uncertainty. We'd be bored out of our heads. In fact, there wouldn't be much point to it at all. The corporate, governmental, and religious institutions of modern society and their radical counterparts rely upon our deep-seated fear of uncertainty and our absolute unwillingness to admit this fear. Without our fear, they are nothing. They know that we desperately want someone else to tell us what the fuck is going on.

Don't give in.

We're so addicted to certainty that we create and obsess over our daily routines. Even though they create the very boredom we complain about. Even though it is these routines, along with our fear of uncertainty, that are the hands that secure the blinders in place on our heads. And those things make it really hard to fully experience life. Don't buy in. Don't sell yourself out. The big lie is that you need to give up your curiosity, your creativity, your desire to cut your own path through life, in the name of becoming an adult. Your curiosity is not the enemy. Any more than terrorism is the enemy. To paraphrase Edward Snowden, bathtubs and police officers kill more people than terrorism, yet we've been told to give up our fundamental rights in order to protect ourselves. It's a lie, just like the lie that it's time to grow up and kill your dreams.

We do not need to cast away our curiosity in order to be fully evolved adults. In fact, it's just the opposite. All of the greatest spirits who have walked the planet have been possessed of fiercely curious minds and hearts. If you are paying attention, there is never a reason to be bored. Wake up. That's it, really. If we are awake, we cannot help but be curious. Because what is curiosity, really, except the tendency to be awake. And to be looking for more stones to turn over.

To be like a child again.

II

LOST & Found

7

THERE ARE DAYS

Nothing real can be threatened. Nothing unreal exists.
—A Course in Miracles

THERE ARE DAYS WHEN THE WORLD will break your heart. I don't mean you will be sad or disappointed or even angry. I don't mean your feelings will be hurt or you will sob into a pillow. I don't mean you will be so depressed you won't want to get out of bed or talk to anyone.

I mean there are days when your heart will break. It will bleed out right on the desk, the floor, the kitchen table. And the pain in your chest will be so great you'll think you cannot bear it. And everywhere you look, everything you read, every conversation you have will feel like peroxide being poured onto an open wound. I mean that you will not be able to see any future that is habitable, because everything will seem irreparably broken. The meanness of the human race will appear beyond comprehension.

There are days when what you believed to be innocent things will suddenly appear as the opposite of what you thought. When the destructive nature of children and their inhumane treatment of one another, suddenly will explain all the world's woes. And you will realize that everyone you know is just a child in grown up clothes, with more responsibilities than they are capable of handling, throwing the occasional toddler's tantrum that is disguised as either righteous indignation or hormonal vicissitudes. And you will understand that their poor treatment of other humans is exactly the same thing as the oversized playground bully making the younger kids cry with his taunting and name-calling.

There are days when the rich will keep getting richer, the greedy greedier, the hard-working even more marginalized, and the sick more in debt. When the insurance companies will continue to steal our money, month after month. When the banks will take our houses and then take some more. And when Congress and our President will seem impotent to do anything about it. Meanwhile they will handover our lunch money to the oil companies, the garden to Monsanto, and whatever is left to the NRA, you know, for protection.

There are days when the world is just mean. That is all there is. Meanness. And the occasional bout of insomnia which shakes us from our chronic slumber of unawareness to acknowledge our inability to do anything about it just before we fall asleep again, exhausted.

There are days where the world will not only break your heart, but tear it out of your chest, stomp on it, and set it on fire, right before your dumbstruck eyes. And you won't know what to do.

And I won't know what to tell you to make it any better.

And yet somehow, somehow, you will find a different set of days. In those days, the sun will be warm on your skin. But there will be just enough cloud cover to allow the colors all around you to show themselves. And your world will be filled with beauty. You'll get buzzed by a hummingbird on your morning walk. And the green and yellow foothills will spread their beauty across the horizon as if just for you.

These are the days that are true. This is what is real. All else is nonsense dreamt up by small minds and feeble imaginations. All else is illusion. All else is the emptiness of delusion.

Come with me. Let's find our own way out. Let's live all our days saturated in beauty.

8

GRAPPLE

Go on. Wrestle that angel.

Lean into her with your whole self. Wrap your arms around and press your torso to hers. Dig in with your heels and feel her weight pressing back. Hold on tight to her arms, her ribs, the curve of her hips, anywhere you can find purchase. Feel her electric pulse course through you. Don't give up. Don't give in. Don't let go too soon.

Our struggles are not curses. They are not mythical demons or punishments for our sins. They are not troubles to be wished away, not obstacles to avoid. There is not another, safer path we should have taken. They are gifts. The trouble is we are conditioned to believe that gifts are only things that come in boxes with wrapping paper and bows. (Or these days, in the last-minute three-dollar bag with colored tissue paper stuffed in the top.)

We're not used to gifts looking like a dark room with furniture we can't see. Let alone a gift looking like our own darkness. Hell, we're not even used to acknowledging our own darkness. Other people's, sure. We're like forest rangers with binoculars on lookout towers when it comes to spotting (and calling out) anyone else's shadow. With any hint of our own shadows tucked up neat and tidy underneath us as we lounge in the brightness of our perpetual high noon. Only rainbows, unicorns, and smiley faces here.

Whatever.

Here's the thing. We're humans. We're not angels, seraphim, or saints. We're not even ascended beings. (If you are actually an ascended being, my apologies.) Which means we don't generally spend our days floating around on clouds, wrapped in unearthly light, singing with voices like gelato (real Italian gelato, I mean), possessing all divine knowledge, and carrying tiny messages of truth to the besotted masses.

As humans, we're possessed of just enough wit to want to know what the angels are talking about, but not quite enough to actually understand them. (You can see why we'd want to wrestle them. They piss us off.) If it feels like this is an unfair situation, that's because it is. And if you think about it, no one promised us anything about life being fair. (Seriously, look on the back of your ticket if you don't believe me.) Life is an enter-at-your-own-risk event.

So, how again are these things supposed to be gifts? Let me explain a different way. Recently there was a single mobile game app from Japan that grossed up to $75 million a month. The worldwide video game industry grossed over $93 billion the same year. What this means is that, while we complain constantly about the riddles of our real lives, we are perfectly willing to spend hard earned cash, and lots of it, to solve make-believe problems. Or at least to blow them up.

Let me say that another way.

You know how, whenever you are part of any given organization—be it your job, your math club, or your cult—someone will eventually decide the thing that will make this group more cohesive is a ropes course? Before it became kind of a cliché, a ropes course was actually a good idea. It allows people to face their fears and to transcend them, generally with the support and encouragement of other humans who are there to face their own demons. The challenges are physical and emotional. And overcoming them provides self-assurance and an opportunity to bond with others.

Life's kind of like that. We don't think of it that way, because life is something we do every day all day, not just once, or once every few years. Whenever I have traveled in my life, I wake up every morning excited to face the unknown adventures that await me. When I am back to my daily routines, I strive to remember that I can greet every day just like this. I don't have to be in another city or country to find adventure or to be excited about my day.

Whether we admit it or not, we like puzzles. We like to be challenged. And not just on the screen. If you think about it, life would probably not be worth living if all the streets were flat, the weather was always perfect, our kids were always well behaved, our thoughts were never troubled, and we had all the money we could ever spend. Wait a second, that actually sounds pretty damn good. Forget all that other stuff I said.

Just kidding.

While it's tempting to think that a life of nothing but ease would be nothing but grand, this is flawed thinking. The only reason we know anything about ourselves is because we've had to figure it out. Stop me if I've said this before, but how many of us have known trustafarians who are pretty screwed up. Probably everyone. Though it may sound like a good idea, saving your children from certain hardships, setting them up so they'll never have to work to make a place for themselves in the world is not really doing them any favors.

So give yourself permission to grapple. It's okay that we don't have everything figured out. It's okay that we walk around daily bearing the weight of these small worlds. That our minds are constantly working on these puzzles in the background. That these angels we wrestle make guest appearances in our dreams, our work lives, our arguments with friends and lovers, our endless conversations with ourselves.

We were born to wrestle. It's part of our DNA. And history tells us the angels know how to lose. So go on. Lean in.

9

BENEFIT OF THE DOUBT

Doubt everything. Find your own light.
—Buddha

SOCRATES MADE HIS STUDENTS ANSWER THEIR OWN QUESTIONS. Galileo dared to doubt the church. And Darwin later took up his legacy. The Buddha described his own path, but wanted people to find their own way. Even Jesus was a man of doubt. If not for the doubters, we'd all still be in Plato's cave.

From Rumi to Rimbaud, the great poets have always been doubters. From Da Vinci to Descartes, our great thinkers have looked through the lens of doubt and reimagined the world.

Bad things happen whenever we excuse doubt from the table at decision time. Without courage to doubt the President, we get a ten-year, two trillion-dollar war. Without courage to doubt our bankers, we see the collapse of a world economy.

If you would be a real seeker after truth,
it is necessary that at least once in your life you doubt,
as far as possible, all things.
—Descartes

If faith is the vehicle to carry one's vision to fruition, then doubt is the bridge upon which it travels. Blind faith is as destructive a force as self-doubt. Both are out of balance and misplaced.

A certain measure of faith is necessary and constructive. We must believe in ourselves, our purposes, our relationships with each other and with the universe, in order to be whole. This faith cannot exist in a vacuum, though, or it becomes a senseless and destructive force that is counter to its essence.

Faith in the unknown, the invisible, the passion which moves us is as essential as oxygen to the human experience. Indeed a full human life is not possible without it. Still faith must know its split-apart doubt, in order to serve us.

> *Faith keeps many doubts in her pay. If I could not doubt, I should not believe.*
> –Henry David Thoreau

Yes, doubt has its place. We are supposed to question, it makes our faith authentic. Those who are afraid to question their beliefs tacitly admit the weakness of them. Those unwilling to acknowledge the possible validity of truths beyond their own become rigid to the natural flows of life.

If we were to peek behind the flimsy curtain, instead of strength, we'd see fragility. If we were to read between the lines of these manifestos, the ink would reveal dogmas, not truths. A building that is too inflexible will crumble when the Earth shifts her weight. A tree that cannot bend will break into pieces in the wind.

So is the mind like these things. When we travel the same thought paths too often, it creates ruts of thought, action, belief. Soon we are limited by where we can go, because the wheels of our brain cannot escape these ruts. Just as we do yoga to keep our bodies flexible, so we need to bend our brains to keep them useful.

> *Perfect confidence is granted to the less talented*
> *as a consolation prize.*
> —Robert Hughes

I doubt any of us were put on this earth to accept someone else's story without a question. We were not given such wonderful brains only to follow instructions. We were not built with an innate sense of our own path just to follow a broken compass someone else gave us. We were not handed a blank piece of paper to color in someone else's lines.

If life is a daring adventure, as Ms. Keller told us, then we must not squander the chance to explore. I would rather doubt and be wrong than blindly accept and be right. At least the misjudgment would be my own.

The aphorisms of the ages are filled with encouragement to step to the beat of your own drummer. There has never been anything memorable written about following convention. No soul was ever inspired by lines teaching that life is about following orders.

> *You are never dedicated to something*
> *you have complete confidence in.*
> *No one is fanatically shouting*
> *that the sun is going to rise tomorrow.*
> –Robert M. Pirsig

Part of the magic of life exists in the balance of many forces that appear, falsely, to be opposites: beauty and decay, love and hate, fear and courage, light and dark, life and death. This is part of the great illusion.

We must believe and doubt in balance or else neither has value. If we are to build the new world, then like an old married couple who've lost their rhythm, faith and doubt must learn to dance again. Let's commit ourselves in the coming days and weeks to learn some new steps.

And to never lose our faith in the power of doubt.

10

FINDING BEAUTY IN DARKNESS

The Russian novelist Fyodor Dostoyevsky not-so-famously said, "Perhaps it is beauty that will save us in the end." I couldn't agree more. And I wrote a piece for Rebelle Society in 2013 on why our most important job is to find beauty. It was true then and it is true now.

I've written before how the world is broken, in many, many ways. And how it is also beautiful. And that we should focus more on the beauty. And I have been criticized for saying that kind of thing, because people mistook it for some kind of spiritual bypass, or they said it was born of white privilege. But despite this criticism, I have never been one to shy away from the full picture. So let's talk about the broken parts for a minute. Let's not shy away or paint glossy pictures of unicorns with rainbows coming out of their nether regions. Let's talk about the state of our modern world.

As I write this, we are still reeling from the mass shooting in Vegas. The one where one shooter with an arsenal of 23 guns, including semi-automatics and hundreds and hundreds of rounds of ammo, caused unimaginable pain, injury, death, and chaos. By the time you read this, the talk of reasonable gun control may have quieted, and the great majority of the nation may have gone back to sleep. But I hope not. I hope that we are all still talking about how we can fix the many things that are broken in our country. Because the way I see it, they are all connected.

I'll start with a list of what I see is broken, those things I believe have contributed to the state of our world. The poverty, the crime, the mass anxiety and hopelessness, and the every-other day mass shootings, as well as other catastrophes, including the 2008 financial crisis from which we are still recovering:

1. *Unfathomable disparity in income distribution.* We do not live in a free market. The US grants something like $125 billion or more a year in corporate welfare. And that does not include tax loopholes and offshore accounts. Meanwhile more than 43 million Americans live in poverty. There are 6 heirs to the Wal-Mart fortune who have amassed more wealth than over 100 million Americans. This is not because they are smarter or work harder or are just luckier. It is a rigged system. Add to this the fact that because those 6 people do not pay their full time employees a living wage, our tax dollars must pay for those employees' food stamps. To the tune of $6.2 billion. In another not-so-far-off time, where we weren't all distracted by our smart phones and social media approval, we'd be marching with torches to tear down their walls. And there would be guillotines waiting.

2. *A Congress filled with people who do not give a shit about you.* Sure, there are outliers: Franken, Sanders, Warren. But mostly Congress cares about getting re-elected and amassing secret wealth on the side that they do not need to disclose while they refuse to pass legislation preventing them from capitalizing on insider knowledge. The NRA, big banks, big insurance, big oil, and their ilk have each of them by the balls. If you don't believe me, just look at Paul Ryan and crew's numerous recent efforts to give billionaires tax cuts while throwing millions of Americans off health care.

It is hard for my mind to wrap around how absurd this is. Mostly because of the fundamental truth that billionaires do not need tax cuts. They wouldn't even notice them. Which leads me to the real problem, which is not greed and corruption, but figuring out why we haven't risen up against this nonsense. Why is it that vast numbers of Americans, who will not benefit from these policies, will likely still re-elect most of these politicians next term. We must correct this problem before any other progress can be made.

3. #45. Look, I sort of get his selling point for some people. We are sick of business as usual in Washington, D.C. and elsewhere in politics. (See numbers 1 and 2, above.) We want big change. We want to break the system into tiny pieces and rebuild it. But this guy was never going be the solution. This guy is the problem. He is the poster boy for The Sociopathic Capitalists Society (except for the ironic fact that he has apparently been propped up by a communist mafia since the 90s). But more troubling than

that, he seems to be a bona fide moron on just about every topic there is. Even more troubling than the fact that he doesn't know things, as George Will noted, is the fact that he does not seem to know what it is to know something. That so many millions of people voted for him, and that so many numbers continue to support him, despite his daily incompetence, is disheartening to say the least, and frankly beyond comprehension;

4. *The archaic, dysfunctional, and misguided judicial system.* We have a Supreme Court who has perpetuated many of our current problems. Including decisions that: (1) grossly misinterpret the second amendment as to allow the NRA to continue its bullying and to allow Americans to stockpile lots of guns that are designed only to kill many, many people very, very quickly. Say from the 32nd floor of a hotel; or (2) the one that equates money with speech and has allowed big money to take over our elections; or (3) the one that gave away the Presidency to a guy who lost the election. And then there is the obvious problem of privately-owned prison systems. And if you can't see the problem with that, just consider how these people would make money if the prisons weren't full. And what a conflict of interest that is for the so-called departments of justice. And consider that the majority of people in federal prison are there for non-violent drug offenses. Many of which are for drugs that are now legal in several states;

5. *Our belief in otherness.* Despite the infuriating reality of the first four enumerated paragraphs, this is probably the most

troubling. From religions, to skin colors, to languages, it seems it is human nature to fear what we do not understand, what is different from us and how we do things. And maybe there is some anthropological good cause for this. But we have greatly exaggerated its usefulness in the modern era. It is time to build bridges to each other, not walls. Our prejudices far outweigh our curiosity, and we need to flip that.

Maybe you knew someone affected by the Mandalay Bay shooting in Vegas. Maybe just the pure senselessness of it shook you. Whatever the case, how many wake up calls do we need? How many times, after the immediate shock of another mass shooting, another financial collapse, another election of a dangerous and willfully ignorant sociopath, another avoidable environmental disaster, another murder of an unarmed black man, another attempted racially-motivated travel ban, will we roll over and hit the snooze button? We must demand more from ourselves and our leaders.

And though it may seem counter-intuitive, one of the things we must demand of ourselves is that we spend more time finding beauty in the world. And also more time creating it. Because finding and creating beauty will, without a doubt, change you and the world.

As I have written before:

We have stacked so much rubbish on top of ourselves, that our true beauty, and the beauty of everyone and everything are buried under our prejudices, our beliefs, our pages and pages of worn out stories. Dig yourself out. Brush yourself off. Throw away the never-ending manuscript of why you can't.

The world is neither this thing nor that thing. It is not our ideas of how it is or of how it should be. The world is the world. Like love, the world contains all possibilities. All darks and lights, all ups and downs, all rainbows of doubt and joy, hardship and pleasure. But I want you to forget all that.

Your job is to find beauty.

11

THE UNKNOWABLE WORLD

Last night I dreamt of the ocean. In all its endless mystery. Of setting out into its wilderness on the journey of a lifetime. Of being on a large ship, in charge of the mast, full of hope and courage. Buoyed by the adrenaline of adventure. And also feeling utterly ill-suited for the task.

What is it about the sea? Its vastness either provokes awe or makes us feel insignificant. Or some combination. Its perfect rhythms offer comfort, but they also drive home how little of this world is within our grasp. The ocean can wash us clean of our earthly cares or—with too little effort to measure—simply wash us away.

The ocean is also a mirror of our human hearts: wild, restless, unyielding, untamable, unknowable. In its reflection there is both inspiration and terror. To admit that our own hearts are so uncharted, so unknowable, despite a lifetime of effort, is more than a little daunting. And also, we know we must continue to try.

There is so much that is beyond us. We cannot know all there is to be known, as we cannot count the waves on the sea. We cannot read all the books in the store, as we cannot love all the lovers to be loved. We cannot solve the riddles of our own hearts, as we cannot count all the grains of sand.

> *He that will learn to pray, let him go to sea.*
> —George Herbert

We are in perpetual need of getting out of our own ways, of getting out of our own heads, of surrendering to that which we cannot know, of letting go of the rocks and the shore and letting the water take us where it will. This, too, is why the ocean calls to us. To share with us its wider view. And to grant us reverence for the one wild and precious life we have been given.

Just as we have drawn imaginary lines to define nations and states, so we have created imaginary boundaries in our own lives, our own hearts and minds. And while some of these made-up borders allow us to get up, make the coffee, put on our shoes, and go about our days, they also keep us from the natural human wandering that is required in order to rediscover the magic of just being alive.

Just as I was enthusiastic for a dream journey that I was also completely unprepared to take, so we walk out into every day of our lives. We ignore the fact that we live in a world that is overwhelmingly designed for things with gills. Not to mention that even that vast world floats on an almost imperceptible wave of the universe's unknowable sea. Maybe it is because our brains can't grasp the size of these mysteries that we ignore the greatness of this wonder as we stumble through each day. Or maybe we spend too much time asleep when we think we are awake.

> *All of us have in our veins the exact same percentage*
> *of salt in our blood that exists in the ocean.*
> –John F. Kennedy

So continues the taunting paradox of the universe. Perhaps it's the ocean's great size which makes it all the more poignant that we are both profoundly lost and found in its presence. Even in its memory.

There is not a thing in the world that does not feel the tug of the sea. Though it seems there are some of us more built for adventure than others. Some who have no choice but to seek out the sea. And still more who cannot be content to simply walk its shores and gaze on its beauty, but must be out in it, as close to part of it as humanly possible. And they cannot imagine any other life. They would not feel whole without it. So it is with our lives on land. Some of us are more willing to take the risk on our dreams.

The ocean is the great metaphor of unknowing, the great mystery, the divine feminine, the collective unconscious, the land of dreams. So a dream about the ocean is then a dream within a dream. A dreamer lost in himself. Out in a universe of fluid borders. Where we are free to dream new worlds into being.

12

LESSONS FROM MY SON

WAKE UP WITH ENTHUSIASM. Especially on the weekends, when those around you would prefer to be sleeping. Open their door as soon as the faintest amount of pre-dawn light is perceptible, and say, in your cheeriest and loudest morning voice, "Time to wake up! It's morning! Who wants to come play?" And then refuse to leave the bedroom until someone agrees to get up with you. Actually, the agreement alone is not enough; history has taught you that these people will say just about anything to get you to leave their room so they can have a few more seconds of rest. You must be adamant that one of them has to come with you. Just sit down and wait, asking every, say, seven seconds or so if they are ready yet. Once you succeed in separating at least one big person from their sleep, bed, sense of peace—and by all means before they can ingest any caffeine—be sure to riddle them with as many questions as possible. And present them with multiple options in a row for your entertainment: "Do you want to build this car kit? Ok, let's do this Lego helicopter. What if we make a gnome village? Or would you rather have a pillow-fight? Or... Dad, you don't have to yell."

Continue to create and recreate the world around you.

If the world around you doesn't look exactly like you want it to, then you just have to make some adjustments. Those adjustments might look like structures made of rocks and mud and pinecones (in the house, of course), or beads and yarn and leaves and acorns that you have collected for years, all strung together in a complex maze throughout your room (or maybe someplace more public, say, the kitchen), or a compilation of every stuffy you own stacked together with every pillow in the house and built just on the inside of your bedroom door, where no one will be able to enter or exit your room without dismantling it completely, and of course there is the quintessential living room fort, which requires you to collect every blanket in the house and to rearrange every stick of furniture in a 50-foot radius and then re-imagine them all as walls and ceilings and hidden paths for your secret lair.

Be a force of nature.

What are you going to do with your one wild and precious life? Anything you can get away with. Anything. Beware any mere mortal who dares to stand in your path, attempt to redirect your energy, or be foolish enough to say the word, *no*.

Be generous with your gifts.

Make stuff for your friends and family as often as possible. Make sure that what ever you are making includes at least five different materials, including glue, glitter (and as often as possible, glitter glue), tape, staples, crayons, colored pencils, markers, paint, colored paper, and material scraps (including old clothes from your parents, or clothes you at least believe are old). Always feel free to borrow from other projects already in progress throughout the house, including leaves, rocks, acorns, pine needles, yarn, and paper scraps. Always use your parents' best scissors to cut your materials (those *craft* scissors they gave you are crap). Make enough crafts for everyone in your class and bug your parents endlessly until they help you spell each of your friend's names for the tags.

Demand more from life.

Don't settle for gifts only on designated holidays or birthdays. Demand that life give you gifts almost daily. Especially if you find yourself within 100 yards of a store of *any* kind. Rinse and repeat.

Question everything.

And I mean absolutely everything that anyone (especially one of your parents) tells you. There is a whole lot of bad information out there. And young children are especially tapped into this phenomenon. In fact, consider setting up your own fact-checking organization, because no one is as relentless at arguing the accuracy of alleged facts than young children.

Play hard.

Do not settle for anything less than sweaty, muddy, wet, stained, leaf and grass-covered, pant-torn (preferably both knees), skin-abrased, stolen-candy-fueled, screaming, toy-abusing, climbing-higher-than-you-know-you-should-on-any-available-tree-or-structure, tennis shoe-thrashing, yard-destroying, neighbor-disturbing, just-shy-of-parent-coronary-causing fun.

Stay in your pajamas as long as possible.

This is the number one rule of all time. All other rules could fall by the wayside to save this one thing. Also, the more the other rules can be combined with this one, the better. Torn and mud-stained pajamas are a sign of the ultimate victory.

III

NEW WORLD
& Old Rubble

13

BUILDING THE NEW WORLD

THE POET MURIEL RUKEYSER once explained that *the universe is made up of stories, not atoms.* I believe her for a number of reasons. Not the least of which is that each atom is a universe unto itself. Each with its own story.

If the universe is made up of stories, then our world is no different. Its own atoms endlessly telling their own stories. Each one as urgently as if it had never been told. Even if no one is listening.

Because no story is ever told in vain. Every word we utter changes the world. One small word whispered into a night sky while lying in a field of stars and staring up into eternity changes forever the landscape into which it ascends.

Forever and ever. Every word. Every moment. Every day. From seven billion mouths and growing. And there is nothing more real than this. Nothing.

Every single word is powered by light and matter, born of will, and infused with all the sound and fury of galaxies colliding in space. Every single word. String them together and it is difficult to comprehend what you have unleashed.

As the poet Joy Harjo once said, *you who thought you could say nothing, write poetry.* Yes, you. Your words are poetry whether you believe it or not. Whether you understand it or not.

The world is made up of stories. And stories are made up of voices. Your voice and mine. And billions of other peoples' voices we don't know and will never meet. We are all creating the world together.

And that seems like a pretty important task. One that we ought to maybe pay greater attention to than we do.

Those of us who regularly sit down to channel words understand the importance of them. But even we fuck it up when it comes to the use of them in our daily lives.

We curse in traffic. We yell at our kids. We tell half-truths and whole lies. We wallow in self-pity. We disparage our neighbors. We rage against the powers that be. We utter whole paragraphs of disbelief and chapter upon chapter of despair.

What other world could we live in than this one, then. With all our rage and our woes, our clever deceit and our self-fulfilling strife, the volumes of chaos that we utter every day.

You heard me right. You and I are responsible for this madness.

And we are also responsible for every beautiful thing that has ever come to be. You and me. Us. We are one in this. Co-creators of the common ecstasy of life, the universe, and everything.

And that everything includes love. Because of course it does. Because love is the source of everything, the DNA of the Universe. The building blocks of life. Remember:

> *love is a word.*
> *love is the word.*
> *love writes its own story.*
> *love writes you in.*
> *—from words: study 8,*
> *Waking Up at Rembrandt's*

Once you are in, once you have taken on this breath, as Harjo puts it, that's it, the story has begun. And there's no getting off the page. We are at work building the new world, as fast as our words can carry us.

It is time to invite the world out for coffee and a new conversation. Let's pretend we don't know each other. Let's ask new questions. Let's put down our phones. Let's take good notes.

In crafting a poem for a new world, we must learn when to speak and when to be silent. Until we have reset the rhythmic pattern and flow of the universe. Until our stories have filled it to the brim with the beauty of living these lives of light and clay.

The world is made up of stories. And stories are made up of voices.

Join me. Let's build the new world.

14

OPEN

Your minds to what I am about to say.

I am not here to hand you another overwrought cliché for you to toss into your growing stack of inspirational quotes you'll forget by dinnertime. I'm talking about changing the way you see the world around you. About rethinking your interactions with that world.

It's not just about your heart.

Sure, being open requires an open heart. And I promise I'll get to that. But first we need to talk about the mind. We all live such a ridiculous amount of time there that the mind is the first door we need to get through.

It would be easy to blame our modern habits. How, increasingly, every spare second of waking life is spent in a frenzy of multi-task-driven dysphoria. But it isn't technology's fault. It's what we do with it. It's how we do what we do with it.

While our technological abilities are growing like a virus on, well, virus steroids, our minds are being numbed into submission. Our minds are constantly opening to new ways to use technology and steadily closing to almost everything else.

The mind and technology have one primary thing in common. They both are meant to work for us. Instead, we end up working for them. To be open means that sometimes we have to stop. We have to put down our electronic addictions and rethink every thing in our lives we have put on autopilot.

Though your heart is essential.

What can be said about the heart that hasn't already been said? Plenty, I'm sure. Because the heart knows everything the mind has ever learned and forgotten. And so much more. The heart has a stash of secrets so large it has taken thousands of years of poets just to reveal a tiny few.

Yes, it is counter-intuitive.

Because everywhere, all day long, there are reasons to close down. To protect yourself. From the naysayers and the nit-pickers, the needy and the ne'er-do-wells. What you cannot see with your heart slammed shut is that everywhere, all day long, there are millions of reasons to stay open. And I'm not just talking about the birds and the butterflies, the sexy storms and the saturation of colors under Sierra clouds. But when you open a door for yourself, you open a door for others.

Find your door to freedom.

Because that is the only way. Because until we are open, we are not free. While we are vigilantly patrolling the borders of our egos, our comfort zone, our I-don't-want-others-to-know-I'm-human, we are missing out on real life.

The battle between open and closed is not new. Its roots are ancient and are still deeply embedded in the modern world. From the oppression of religious theocracies to the free love and new age movements, this tension between open and closed remains a central theme of life.

I get it. The world can be a scary place. But the secret to freedom is the same as the secret to conquering dream monsters. You must turn and look them in the face. Though you're afraid of whatever may be on the other side of the door, you must open it anyway.

This is the only way to freedom. You must open doors. Everywhere, every day, all the time. Open the door to smiling at strangers. Open the door to asking him out. Open the door to admitting mistakes. Open the door to saying you're sorry. Open the door to letting more go.

And then open a little more.

I'm talking about standing on desks. About challenging your thoughts, your feelings, your fears, your ideas, your knowings, your ways.

You may think you're already there. You're already open and out there. But I'll bet you a beer you're not. I'll bet that you could add a million tiny freedoms to your life that take no time or money.

Open to the idea of rain, to the possibilities of flowers. Open to the rush of your real life lived, not simply imagined. Open your skin to the touch of a lover. Open your arms to your friends. Open your wallet to a stranger. Open your chakras, your mantras, and your ideas of yourself.

There will always be naysayers. Open the door and let them go. Let go of all your collected thoughts of you. And make room for the joy that will flood itself in as soon as you unclutter your you.

Swim naked.

Because really, is there anything better? Then do it in everything you do. Strip off the layers of closed-door clothes and dive in. Feel the silky caress down the length of your life. And live all the secrets of you.

Let yourself unfold like all the flowers of spring. Give yourself and your beauty to the world. And then let the world shine it right back on you.

15

TRUST

As if you'd never been betrayed. There's a reason we still read Shakespeare after all this time. He understood that betrayals come in all forms. Betrayal of county, of friends, of family, of love and lovers, of yourself. If you are surprised by that last one, perhaps you haven't been paying enough attention.

Trust. As if you didn't know better.

While we walk around guarding ourselves against every conceivable threat from the outside, most of us betray ourselves in small and big ways all day, everyday. Mostly it's the little voice that we carry around inside us. The one that nags, criticizes, and unnecessarily narrates our lives all day long. (And all night for those insomniacs among us.) Once we turn on the light of awareness, we realize that all this listening we do to this sociopathic voice in our heads is exhausting.

Trust. As if you'd never been burned.

We never really get used to being let down. By ourselves, our friends, our government, those we place on pedestals. Yes, there is a place for discretion. But more often then not, our mistrust sets in motion a negative cycle. Call it phenomenology or whatever you like, but all things are connected. How we look at others has a direct correlation not only with how they see us, but how they act towards us. If we start with our hearts open, we'll likely not attract the spirit of betrayal.

Trust. As if no one would ever be the wiser.

Trust does not come without risk. This is not a story of unicorns and rainbows. Life is risk. The only way to protect ourselves is to die. Either physically, or spiritually and emotionally. I believe, with the exception of a Caesar or two, we are not so much afraid of betrayal as we are of looking foolish, of getting our feelings hurt, our egos bruised, our so called reputations tarnished. If it helps, next time you are doubting whether to trust your heart, pretend no one is watching. Pretend you fell on the ice and got up before anyone saw. Because, probably no one will know anyway. And it is likely no one will care half as much as you do.

Trust. As if your life depended on it.

Because, well, it does. What is the value of a life where you have to walk around constantly checking your back like some meth dealer in an alley? Hopefully that is rhetorical. Unless of course you're a meth dealer who dwells in alleys. And then, well, you have other problems besides trust. Except it wouldn't hurt for you to trust that you are worth more than this and to trust that life has infinitely more to offer.

Trust. As if there were no other choices.

Because, well, there really isn't a better choice. We must trust, on some level, in order to function at all in life. Every day we trust in a million little ways. Not just that the lights will work, the water will flow, the car will start, the garbage will be picked up, the bank won't give away your money. But also that the thousands of cars we pass will stay in their own lanes, that gravity will continue to work, that our hearts won't forget to beat, that we won't have to remind our lungs to breathe.

Trust. As if it were as essential as oxygen.

We do not give trust its due. Like oxygen, we file away its importance until we are under water. Until we are frightened and our hearts have already slammed shut. And then there's little chance we'll remember. But the unspoken truth is that it is trust, not fear, that makes the world go 'round. If fear were the order of the day, if vigilance were the reigning factor, then nothing would get done. The richest of people on the planet trust countless others all day long, every day. Neither Gates nor Jobs, nor Musk nor Oprah built their empires on their own. We rely upon countless others every day for more things than we can count. Look at that sandwich you are eating. Who grew the grains for the bread, the vegetables, the mustard seeds? Who milked the cows and who cultured the cheese? Who salted and hung the prosciutto? Who mined the metals and built the toaster? Who welded the steel counter where the ingredients were assembled? If we did not trust in these processes, we'd never take a bite.

Trust. As if to do anything else would be unthinkable.

When we throw away trust, we throw away our key to the door of humanity. We perpetuate more of the violence we inflict regularly upon ourselves and others with our misinformed judgments and our withheld compassion. There is no one who is not deserving of your compassion, starting first with yourself. When we have compassion for ourselves, we find it easier to have compassion for others. When we show and are shown compassion, trust naturally follows. When we trust, we retrieve the key to the door, and once opened, life's abundance is allowed to flow inside.

16

DIG DEEPER

It's these expressions I never give
That keep me searching for a heart of gold.
—Neil Young

I'VE LISTENED TO NEIL sing that song maybe a thousand times. (Raise your lighters if you know what I'm talking about). And so, naturally, I thought I understood what it was about. It's a theme song for every soulmate-searcher on the planet, right? It's a lyrical manifesto for every sensitive romantic looking for The One. You know, the search for the glass slipper's perfect fit, the twin flame, the split-apart, the heart of gold.

Sure, that's part of it. But if you read the quote at the top of the page again, you'll discover it's not just a story of the search for true love. We've all done our share of mining. And we've all come up short of our expectations. Is that because we were looking in the wrong places? Or were we looking for the wrong things?

I won't pretend to have a backstage pass to Neil's psyche. But I think he was trying to explain that he didn't have to go to Hollywood or to Redwood (or across the ocean) to complete his search. He confessed that he'd been spending too much time in his mind. (It's such a fine line.) And as everyone knows, no good has ever come from that.

So what's a determined glass slipper-bearer to do? I'm not going to tell you that you need to make yourself into the kind of person who would be lovable by the kind of person you want to find. Because other people have probably told you that. I'm happy to remind you it's true. But that's not the end of the story.

The crux of the tale, I think, was best told by Sam Phillips: *We don't want lives of steel / We don't want hearts that feel / We want to live above it all.* At first glance, these two lyrical stories don't appear to cohabitate very well. But if you listen a little closer, they're both saying the same thing. The hard truth is that you won't find a heart of gold without doing a little work.

If you only want a soulmate so your life will be cushier, well, I've got some bad news. Life's not really like that. If you want a heart that doesn't feel any pain, then you're not going to have a heart of gold. And if you don't have a heart of gold, well, you're not likely to find a heart of gold.

The key is in the first line of Neil's quote, "It's these expressions I never give" that keep him searching. In other words, he needs to get out of his mind and out of his own way. He says he wants to live and he wants to give, but he's not doing the latter, so he can't do the former.

Hearts of gold don't find themselves lined up at the doorstep of those unwilling to give anything of themselves. And I'm not taking about the desperate kind of neediness that disguises itself as having just so much love to "give." I'm talking about being willing to live your own life. About being authentic. And about still being strong enough to share that life, its gifts, and the space it inhabits, with another human being, heart, soul, and sometimes messy fallout.

Real life is not neat and clean. Life is about digging in and getting yourself dirty. Look around at the people who are happiest. You'll see they aren't worried about mud. Because without a little mud, life is not possible.

Wanting to live above it all means we never even scratch the surface. And while staying on the surface might keep us clean, it isn't all that interesting, is it? One thing's for sure, we are never going to find any gold just laying around on the surface. That's not where gold likes to hang out.

Gold is a little more secretive than that. Gold is a cat, hiding god knows where until it is ready to be found, snuggling down into its makeshift forts of cardboard and cupboards, bushes and boxes, blankets and pillows. The more layers the better. And there it rests, waiting for our wits to grow sharp enough to find it.

Gold is a playful lover. One who wants you to work a little for it, knowing the payoff will be worth the effort. Yes, gold is kind of like foreplay. And if you think of it more as play than work, you're likely to have a lot more fun.

Hearts, as it turns out, are much the same. Though, from time to time, we've been known to wear them on our sleeves, this is not their preferred location. Hearts prefer to stay deep within our chests, where only those willing to look deep enough will be able to see them.

Hearts of gold are the rarest of metals. And the only way to find a heart of gold is to first transform your own heart. Like attracts like, no matter what you've been told. If you want to live, you've got to give, of yourself and your heart.

You've got to give to yourself and to others. You've got to use your voice and to make space for other voices. You can't stand above it all, like some heartsick Gatsby peering over the balcony. You've got to walk into the crowd, the river, the mud, this thing called life. Yes, you.

Keep turning over stones. And I'll see you in the river.

17

THE HIDDEN WORLD

MUSIC IS KNOWN FOR ITS MYSTERIOUS ability to unlock memories that have been secreted away for years. Somehow it has access to a portal that leads to a hidden world. But that's not where the mystery ends. With just a few lines, a songwriter can tell us many stories. And it's uncanny how often they seem to be about our own lives.

Let me show you an example. Because I don't want to alter your own stories of one of your favorite songs, I chose something a little obscure: the Elton John song *Come Down in Time* (lyrics in bold):

In the quiet silent seconds

[I believe in jazz. I believe that the space between the notes is more important than the notes themselves. I believe in the in-breath. I believe in the power of silence. I believe in the importance of friends who do not have to talk to understand each other. I believe that less is more. And that the most powerful writing lets the reader fill in some blanks.]

I turned off the light switch

[One of my favorite poets, John O'Donohue, reminds us that the soul likes candlelight. And that it's best not to use bright lights when seeking to know ourselves. For me, darkness is also comforting, seductive even.]

And I came down to meet you

[I believe in bridges. I believe that the meeting of two beings -- even though it happens every day, all day, and we mistake it for something commonplace -- contains all the mystical metaphors of life. Everything in the universe is constantly in motion. And everything (ourselves included) is constantly crossing a magic threshold, towards recognition, towards awakenings, towards oneness.]

In the half light the moon left

[There is no such thing as the half moon. And yet this metaphor is everything. We are all whole. And yet we mostly do not see this. And while the moon, like everything in the universe, has its own light, the light we mistake for its own is actually a reflection of something else. Also, the moon not only casts light, but shadows. Just like us.]

While a cluster of night jars

[I had to look this up, long ago. Nightjars are nocturnal birds. They have very small feet and so spend most of their time flying. I just love the way the words sound. There is something enchanting about them I can't explain. Which is another reason to love it. Our desire to explain so many things, instead of simply feeling them, is part of our folly.]

Sang some songs out of tune

[We put too much emphasis on voices being pretty. What a shame if Tom Waits, Bob Dylan, or Neil Young had decided not to sing. Heart is far more important than technique.]

A mantle of bright lights
Shone down from a room

[Light can come from anywhere. And everywhere. Like the importance of silence, this phrase lets us fill in the blanks. It could be a literal upstairs room. Or the room could be the sky. And the mantle of lights the stars.]

Come down in time I still hear her say
So clear in my ear like it was today

[Memory is a mystical thing. Songs, smells, words, sounds, and places all have the ability to transport us back in time. And time is an endless enigma. So much time elapses, and yet, no time at all has gone by, *like it was today*. And longing can bend time—both backwards and forwards—as deftly as any force in the universe.]

Come down in time was the message she gave
Come down in time and I'll meet you half way…

[Even though we are constantly interacting with one another, it is rare that we really meet. We must be present, in the flow, and so grounded that our own gravity lines up the stars. We must meet each other, opportunity, love, and beauty at least halfway. We must build these bridges together. We must remind each other of the oneness inside every split-apart in the universe.]

18

HOW TO BLEND THE WORLDS

The universe is an endless paradox of limited visibility. (How's that for an opening line.) Too often we believe that only this *or* that can be true. That there is such a thing as the truth, the whole truth, and nothing but the truth. That people can only be with us or against us.

From our flawed judicial system to the daily conversations inside and outside our heads, we live in an increasingly thin slice of reality. One in which people, things, and ideas are categorized, stereotyped, and affixed with childish labels like right or wrong, good or bad. A place where, in the name of a loving God, people hate one another.

What all these thoughts and conclusions have in common is the arrogance of believing that the universe is knowable. And that the thinkers of all these thoughts know all there is to know. Think about that. Think about what this mix of certainty and arrogance requires.

The internet both connects us and keeps us separated from one another. Not just because we are glued to our phones instead of physically interacting. It also allows us to be insular in our associations and narrow in our exposure.

Yes, to a certain extent this has always been true. We have long subscribed to the newspapers and magazines that fit our worldview, favored one news channel over another, and stayed steadfastly true to one political party. Technology has simply amplified those tendencies. While also allowing us to avoid anything like an actual conversation.

It's easy to hate on a certain segment of America for not seeing things the way we do. But there's also a kind laziness in that behavior. And a measure of hypocrisy. If we're honest with ourselves, we've all become willfully ignorant to things we find unpalatable or inconvenient, and those blind spots allow us to be unquestionably sure that our conclusions are the right ones.

The marketplace of ideas thrives when people are talking. To each other. Not just to the choir. I'm not talking about opening the corral gate so free speech can lead us to the truth. (See paragraph one.) I'm talking about expanding our ideas (of ourselves and each other), our possibilities, and our humanity.

Like never before, we need to step out of our bubbles and breathe fresh air. We need to understand that America is every gradation of white, black, brown, and orange. We are also young, old, gay, straight, transgender, strong, feeble, smart, dumb, courageous, and confused.

If we look around and all our friends are the same color, religion, or end of the political spectrum, we are part of the problem. We must go out and mingle outside our comfort zones. And while I'm not advocating we go out and make a token gay friend so we can say we're not bigots, why not start with finding that one friend. And then have some real conversations with them. Conversations that are based upon curiosity and not knowing.

In fact, here's my recipe for a happier future: Take one part your ideas and add several parts of the ideas from others around you that you mostly agree with but have not fully explored. Next add another handful ideas you've heard of, but are not so sure about. Blend together and let sit.

Once settled, slowly add equal parts ideas you've never heard of and those you think you disagree with. Stir vigorously and put in the oven at low temperature for as long at it takes for you to understand that alone, your ideas are just flour, with maybe a little water sprinkled on top. In order for them to be truly interesting, they need to be combined with other flavors and textures.

Once your batter has turned into something with more substance, remove from the oven and let cool. Then invite over your closest friends, some people you know, but don't really hang out with, then add a few strangers, and those who do not share your political, ethnic, religious, gender, or sexual identity. Slice up the concoction. Set out the plates and glasses. Pour some lemonade, open some wine, and start talking. And listening.

IV

WORDS
&
Their Noticeable Absence

19

THE INGREDIENTS OF WORDS

WORDS CONTAIN QUESTIONS. I know that sounds funny. But it's true. While words give us answers like *who* we are talking about or *where* they are or *how* much they've had to drink, they also contain questions, like *what did he mean by that?* In fact, the very word *what* could be a question or an answer. Words can tell you *what she was wearing* and also leave you wondering, *what's going to happen next?*

Pick a word, any word, and I'll bet you'll see what I mean. Here's a random list: *light, bar, clock, sort, kiss, swim, trace.* Are these words verbs or nouns? [It's time to *sort* the laundry. –or– He's the *sort* of guy you don't want to date.] Are they commands or descriptions? [*Trace* that call! –or—She left only a *trace* of perfume her lover's torso.] Are they meant to be friendly or foreboding? [It was their first *kiss.* –or— That's the *kiss* of death.] I could go on…

Everyday we use hundreds of words without really thinking about their meaning, without even acknowledging the questions. Take the word *illegitimate,* a word that—until very recently—was widely used to indicate a child born of two people who were not married. To me, the unspoken question in this word is, *Really?*

Consider the phrase *Happy Holidays.* It seems innocent enough, a straightforward gesture of goodwill. Apparently though, there are many questions lurking in those two simple words. Enough of them to evoke complaints and pleadings for us to use the words *Merry Christmas* instead, so as not to exclude Christ in the season's greetings. But *Happy Holidays* is meant to *be inclusive* not *exclusive*. It is meant to enfold the Christian celebration along with many others.

The best example of a word that comes with questions is *love*. I think Howard Jones has my back on this when he asks, *What is love, anyway?* The question is not merely lyrical. Love is so vast that it defies explanation. More than this, it begs for questions. Questions which force us to stop and pay attention. To examine ourselves and our actions, our thoughts and feelings, our preconceived notions. Love asks us to reach beyond our ideas of ourselves in order to find bigger answers.

We give honor to words, to ideas, to beliefs, to our common humanity, by acknowledging the things that lie outside our understanding and experience. These questions hidden in words are born of the things that awaken our curiosities, things that form questions on our lips, our hearts, our minds (and possibly other parts of our anatomies). Rigidity is good for things like dams, for objects which need to hold things back, to constrict and restrain. Trees, grasses, flowers, rivers, birds, minds, and spirits, these things need to flow and to bend. Let's acknowledge the questions in our words and ideas of the world. Let's embrace them and take time to discover their secrets.

Or as the master once put it:

Be patient toward all that is unsolved in your heart and try to love the questions themselves.
—Rainer Maria Rilke

20

ELEVATE THE WORD

Young children are not that interested in books without pictures. No matter how good the story. When we are very young, a word on a page, by itself, is just not that interesting. We need pictures to make the words more engaging.

As we grow older, our stories also grow, and there are fewer and fewer pictures. As this happens, another kind of magic takes hold. The words on the page begin to mean something. And we start to participate in the story. We bring our imagination to the page and create our own pictures.

This is because a word is a magical thing. And the reading of words is actually an act of creation. As readers, we get to participate in the art itself coming to fruition like no other art form. We are brought into the world made by the writer and get to do our own co-creating while we're there; completing the circle of art in a way wholly unique to the written word.

Please don't misunderstand me. I love the visual arts. Words and pictures have long worked together. And they've enjoyed a beautiful working relationship. I've just noticed that lately the relationship has become a little lopsided. As if there's been a regression of sorts. At least as far as the internets are concerned.

The truth is, we've gotten a bit lazy. We can't be bothered to write out the full words for things. And in order to get us to read something, there needs to be a picture attached. Its like we're all in kindergarten again, and we're easily bored.

Which is a shame. Not just because I'm a writer. But because the word is fundamental to our understanding of everything in our world. Including pictures. Imagine describing a picture without words. Now imagine seeing a picture and not attaching words to it in your own head.

And the thing is, understanding is pretty important. Because mostly what we understand is so vastly outweighed by what we don't understand that if we understood only that simple truth it would blow our minds. And maybe it would lead to things like humility, compassion, and even curiosity.

In order to understand our world a little better, we need to exercise our brains a little more. Reading is a little like yoga for our minds. And who among us couldn't stand to do a little more yoga, right?

Here's something really crazy. New studies show [I promise this isn't a gum commercial] that our brains might actually see words as pictures. Did you hear that? At least some of us see words as pictures. If that's so, then putting pictures with words might be redundant.

I guess what I'm saying is: In a world that is already increasingly disconnected—and almost unbearably truncated by letters and numbers that are supplanting words—to continue to act as if words themselves are not important is to further distance ourselves from each other and from our natural environment.

It's not just that always supplying the picture is too much spoon-feeding. Nor simply that it doesn't allow us the space to create our own worlds with words. It isn't even that it makes us lazy. It's that it also deprives us of the raw beauty of words.

And beauty, as you know, is just about everything. So bring on the written word, the spoken word, the poetry slams, the calligraphy pens, the handmade paper, the ragged journals, and the tattered book covers holding so many precious gems.

Language existed before the written word. But the written word built bridges for us that language alone could not. Let's get creative and figure out how to lift up the word again. In all its art forms. In all its glory. In all its ravenous beauty.

After all, if a picture is worth a thousand words, why not let the picture speak for itself. And set the words free again.

21

LET'S TALK ABOUT WRITING

THIS IS NOT THE SORT OF THING I DO MUCH, talk about writing. Unless you count one of the main characters in my first novel, or several essays I've written, or unless someone asks and I know they are not just making small talk, or conversations I have over dinner with friends, or if I just feel like talking. But other than that, almost never.

I dance around words. I pretend to hide from sentences. I tease turns of phrase. It takes me days to pick up a pen. I am a writer.

I want to tell you how some days I'm taller than buildings, can stop speeding bullets with my fingertips, carry babies from burning houses, and write my way out of anything and into anything else. Before you make coffee.

But it isn't always that way. Not for me. Probably not for you. Not for anyone else I know.

How can I tell you what it means to be a writer? Imagine you knew nothing of science, how would you describe air or what it feels like to breathe? How would you explain to someone from a dry planet that water is wet, or show the colorblind how the sky is blue.

I scribble masterpieces on matchbooks. I collect sentence fragments like fairy dust. I watch the world through my own kaleidoscope eyes. I am a writer.

To write is to live inside a dream. More than this, it is to be the dreamer and the dream. To live in a limitless world of seamless dimensions. Writing and dreaming share a common language. Both speak in metaphors, the only suitable tongue for this extraordinary experience called life.

I awake from a world of limitless possibilities inside a world of narrow boundaries. I scramble to scribble down the memories of the other side.

You and I are metaphors. Along with all we see and do. There is no explanation for life beyond the dreamworld, beyond what we can learn from poetry and from Zen masters. This world is an illusion, a fact we forget again and again and again.

Buckminster Fuller reminded us, *There are no solids in the universe. There's not even a suggestion of a solid.* Think about that.

To write is to fully embrace the world where the illusion does not matter, a world where things like love defiantly reign supreme. Because love is not the opposite of hate, of fear, of oppression, or inhibition. Love contains all these things and more. This is what Rilke was talking about when he said, *Out beyond ideas of wrongdoing and rightdoing there is a field. I'll meet you there.*

To write is to begin to know. To know is to begin to become.

Once you lose the illusion that love, good, righteousness are on one side, and whatever other thing you can imagine is on the other, then your ears start to open. Then your eyes start to hear. Then you may begin to write.

But make no mistake, that's what it is, a beginning. The dreams of our greatness, they come and they go. The moments of fearless are fickle and slow.

Maybe you'll read these words and either nod or shake your head. Depending on the sun or the moon or the tides. But it may or may not change your world. Because the truth is that there are days we all wonder how we got here. Days we stumble, days filled with fear. Days we look around at the room, wonder who will find us out and how soon.

These things, these thoughts, these soul-crushing doubts, by the way, are how we know we're on the right track.

Without them, without a sense of humility, without some acknowledgement of grace, of magic, of the muse, of the 10,000 hours of practice required, we'll never really inhabit this world. But that's a story for another day. Today we're talking about writing.

Because there is almost nothing better. As Bukowski once reminded us, *you will be alone with the gods, and the nights will flame with fire.*

I spent the better part of ten years writing my first novel, *Waking Up at Rembrandt's*. I say that like I did nothing but sit in a room for ten years and write that novel. That isn't true, of course. Back then I did not have a small child dependent upon me for his livelihood. But I did have a day job, a penchant for travel, a taste for good wine, an epicurean addiction, and when

I wasn't suffering a bout of espresso-induced insomnia, a love of sleep, each of which takes up a lot of time.

The thing is, a writing life is neither glamorous nor easy. And yet, if it is in your veins, no amount of transfusions of normal life will help. So if you are called by these words, I invite you to let go of your resistance and join me. You won't regret it.

As Bukowski also reminded us, *the gods wait to delight in you.*

22

YOU'RE NOT THE BOSS OF ME

we do not create words,
we discover them.

words have their own identities,
their own minds, their own sense of purpose.

–from words: study 5,
Waking at Rembrandt's

Don't tell me what to do. Especially not with words. And whatever you do, don't tell me this word or that one is *yours* and I can't use it.

Who owns a word? I wish that were a rhetorical question, but it isn't. Really, how could anyone actually own a word? Or a combination of words? Or a phrase? A turn of phrase, now maybe we are in different territory. A collection of turns of phrases, now we are in the realm of literature, of art, which most would agree should be protected from piracy in some fashion.

I need to stop before I go any further with this piece and give you fair warning that I don't know a damn thing about intellectual property law. So don't take any of this as legal advice.

As an artist, I believe in the importance of copyrights. I believe it is important to protect the integrity of a work. I also believe it is important to protect the sustainability of art, by facilitating it's financial viability. Perhaps more importantly, I believe a copyright is about proper stewardship of the work in question more than it is about ownership.

Here's the thing though, (if I were king) I would draw the line at corporate ownership of words. And people wouldn't be allowed to put combinations of words in quotation marks under the names of their businesses, either. The last rule is mostly because I just think that's dumb. If you are reading this, and you feel you absolutely must have a tag line for your widget delivery service, just don't put it in quotes.

I read there was a fight a while back over who was going to be able to trademark the words "Occupy Wall Street." Obvious irony aside—what interest do we have in allowing this? To be fair, I suppose it could keep a few people off the unemployment roster. But is that worth it? Because claiming ownership to words like these, and collecting money off their use—while having an undeniable comic value—also seems criminally absurd.

And so what if some brass and marble office in Washington, D.C., with a crumbling facade and squeaky chairs, deems that this or that pairing of words belongs exclusively to Entity X (the entity itself being a kind of fiction—but that is for another piece). As an artist, the idea of faceless corporations owning words and phrases feels like blasphemy. I say we release the words from all their corporate oppressors and let them wander free again.

> *re-examine all you have been told ...*
> *dismiss whatever insults your own soul.*
> —Walt Whitman

23

SOMEDAY WORDS

SOME DAYS IT'S LIKE THAT. You'd rather do just about anything other than write. Go pick out the new ladder you've needed for months, give yourself permission to buy a shop vacuum, hand water your outdoor plants, rearrange your office furniture, go for a bike ride, clean the grill, cut your fingernails, check your Facebook page... again.

And still part of you knows you'd really rather be writing than anything else. If you could just start putting words on the page. If you could find the courage, patience, stillness, to write that first sentence, fragment, title, word.

And sometimes you may chicken out and just move straight to editing. Moving around words that are already there and trying to pretend that it's the same thing. Though you know it isn't.

Or your flow may get interrupted by some random thought, phone call, text message, memory, shiny thing, erotic fantasy. And then it may take you the better part of an hour to make your way back to it. Or it may just be gone. Evaporated into the ether to become condensation on some other writer's water glass.

Some days it's like that. You start with the best of intentions. Or even a bad cliché. But you are conscious of how precious the time is. And you resolve to beat back every other nagging critic telling you there are other responsibilities that need tending to. And still, you hover.

So you allow yourself another espresso. Fuel for the journey, you tell yourself, for probably the thousandth time. And though you know it's a half-truth, you do it anyway. And you're not sure if it will actually help, and you remain feeling guilty and whipping yourself the whole way there and back, but you do it all the same. And you know you'll do it again.

You know the best bet is to start first thing in the morning. Somewhere there aren't friends to talk to or other chores to nag at you. You know that the lie you tell yourself otherwise—that you'll just clear some things off your desk first, and then you'll write—has never been true before. But each day is new, and so you believe this time Lucy won't snatch the football at the last minute. That you'll be able to connect with the ball and to cleanly deliver a true kick through the goal posts.

Later, when you find yourself after midday lying flat on your back in the grass with your head pounding, not having written any actual words, you'll resolve again to get up and get straight to work. There's still a full afternoon left, after all.

And then, on those days where you do sit right down, where the words are there and flowing and real, and all feels right with the universe, and all the wasted writing days, hours, minutes, that have come before suddenly vanish like desert rain, you must not think too much about what you are doing. About what you have done. Because if you do, you may suddenly start to feel self-satisfied about your productivity, which may lead to another thought about what else you may be able to accomplish on this glorious day, which may lead to delusions that you have already accomplished far more than you have, which may lead to thoughts of rewarding yourself with a beer over lunch, which will—if history is any guide—more than likely lead to the end of your word flow for the day.

Writing is more than just sitting down and bleeding at the typewriter. It is also about a lot of pencil sharpening, lying in wait, trying to sneak up on the paper, the pens, the unsuspecting words. It's about tricking yourself into sitting still. It's about playing the role of the medium and surrendering to the trance.

Writing is more than just showing up, though showing up is never as easy as it sounds. Make no mistake, the channeling is hard work. True, there's a rush. But like heroin, it takes its toll on the psyche, and like sex, it's hard to sustain for hours.

Some days it's like this. But when it's not, you can't wait for another day like this.

24

WALKING LESSONS

I SHOULD START BY SAYING that I'm not someone prone to writer's block. In general, I have more ideas than I know what to do with. And more words wanting to get out of my head and onto the paper (or you know, screen) than I generally have time to lead them there. Even as I scribble out this confession, I have no shortage of creative projects on my metaphoric plate. Still, if I'm honest with you (and myself), I've been having a little trouble lately, well, writing. That's not exactly true. The real truth is I'm having a *truckload* of trouble writing. I simply can't seem to usher the words anywhere near to where they need to go. And even when I do, I find myself looking around the room for whoever wrote the banal scratch I'm staring at. And then, more often than not, I close my notebook and go on with my day as if the very world itself were not collapsing around me.

Now, for most people, that would be enough. But actually the terror does not end there. At the same time I'm engaged in this mortal struggle with words, I'm also slightly out of my depth on several other projects: (1) researching a technical subject I know almost nothing about for my next novel; (2) working on material for a non-fiction book and companion workshop; and (3) developing a multi-faceted podcast series. And when I'm not doing one of these stretching exercises, I'm probably watching a master class to evolve my craft, researching one of the hundreds of things I still don't know about marketing and audience building, or falling down the rabbit hole of social media. Oh yeah, I've also got a law practice to run and a bright young boy who stays up nights thinking of ways to keep me on my toes.

As you might guess, on any given day I can find myself feeling less than competent about any or all of these components. And really, all the advice out there on life hacking doesn't help. Those seemingly innocuous self-help bites just reinforce the feeling that I have no idea what I'm doing.

Admittedly, writing is not like most other jobs. It's prone to a unique kind of frustration. Not the least of which is that there have never been any guarantees that the ideas or the words or your focus will all show up when they are supposed to, in any kind of meaningful order. But that is also what makes writing kind of magical.

The thing I'm starting to believe is that the harder I try to *make* any of these things happen, the more I chase the fickle cats of progress or achievement, the more I think I really *need* to do or be some thing, the more these things become water between my fingers. There seems to be an inverse magnetic effect.

I find that when I loosen my grip a little, however, things start to shift. When I practice walking, instead of just getting somewhere, then the view expands. And then what appears on the horizon as I wander these tangled paths of a creative life looks like a hidden meadow, a place where the trees offer quiet shade and the grass wants nothing more than for me to just come lie down.

And so I am learning to walk without expectation of where I'm going to arrive. And to realize how many unnecessary things I've been carrying on this long journey. And to set them down.

V

ART
&
THE
SEARCH FOR
BEAUTY

25

YOUR JOB IS TO FIND BEAUTY

Just stop it, already. You know what I'm talking about. You, telling that same old story about how impossible things are, how unfair. The story of how the whole world is rigged, and not in your favor. The story of inequality, injustice, oppression, corruption, lies. The story of why it is understandable that you are where you are.

I've said it before, this world is imperfect. In fact, in many ways, it's down right broken. But that doesn't mean it's not also beautiful. Your job is not to fix all the problems. Your job is not even to point them out or to explain them.

Your job is to find beauty.

Because it is out there. And it is in here. It is everywhere you look. And it is everywhere you don't look.

> *When our eyes are graced with wonder,*
> *the world reveals its wonders to us. There are people*
> *who see only dullness in the world and that is because*
> *their eyes have already been dulled. So much depends*
> *on how we look at things. The quality of our*
> *looking determines what we come to see.*
> *–John O'Donohue*

Practice what you preach. Better yet, stop preaching. And just be. No one wants to listen to preaching anyway. At least not for very long. And not over and over again. Even if they agree with you.

If you find you are well suited to repairing a small piece of the world that is broken, then by all means, go ahead. We need your services. We need fixers and healers of all shapes and sizes and colors.

But just in case I wasn't clear, I'll say it again.

Your job is to find beauty.

Your job is to seek it out, acknowledge it, share it, nurture it, photograph it, paint it, sculpt it, write about it, draw its name in the sand, scatter its petals over the ocean, light up the night sky with its fire.

As an artist, your job is also to create beauty. To be it. That is the birthright of each and every one of us. To acknowledge our own beauty. To become it. To look beneath the surface, to brush away the dust, to shake out the rugs.

We have stacked so much rubbish on top of ourselves, that our true beauty, and the beauty of everyone and everything are buried under our prejudices, our beliefs, our pages and pages of worn out stories. Dig yourself out. Brush yourself off. Throw away the never-ending manuscript of why you can't.

The world is neither this thing nor that thing. It is not our ideas of how it is or of how it should be. The world is the world. Like love, the world contains all possibilities. All darks and lights, all ups and downs, all rainbows of doubt and joy, hardship and pleasure. But I want you to forget all that.

Your job is to find beauty.

26

SAVE THE WORLD, BUY ART

I'VE SAID IT BEFORE AND I'M SURE I'LL SAY IT AGAIN: Your job is to find beauty.

Yes, your life is messy. Yes, your job is stressful. Yes, your romantic partnership is hanging by a thread. Yes, traffic sucks. Yes, your children won't listen. Or stop talking back. Or stop crying. Or stop leaving Legos and bouncy balls in the middle of the kitchen floor where you'll step on them in the dark and damn near kill yourself. Or them.

Yes, the laundry is overflowing. Yes, you forgot to water your plants. Again. Yes, you blew the deadline. Yes, it will be another year before you can apply again. Yes, the thing you wanted more than anything in the whole universe didn't happen. Or at least it didn't happen to you.

Yes, on top of your personal crazy world of red lights, tax forms, relationship disasters, and impossible financial obligations, all over the world people are doing terrible things to other people. And to animals. And to the planet. Which, as it turns out, is the same thing as doing those things to people and animals. But believe it or not, there is something you can do about it: Buy art.

If you don't believe me, just listen to Picasso, he knows:

> *Art washes away from the soul*
> *the dust of everyday life.*
> *–Picasso*

Sure, you say. I'll just forget about all the world's troubles, and my own, stick my head in the sand mandala, and hide. Well, okay. That's better than a hundred other things you could do. But I don't see it as just hiding. I see it as one of the more powerful things you can do to change the world.

What the hell am I talking about? I'll tell you what. Actually, I'll let Anaïs Nin tell you, because she said it quite nicely: *We don't see things as they are, we see them as we are.*

What I mean, in case you're still scratching your head, is that your life is the sum total of all the things you focus on in a day. Which is why I keep saying your job is to find beauty. Which means your job is also to buy that piece of art that embodies the beauty you seek.

Unless, of course, you want the terrorists to win. Then just sit at home and look at your blank walls, worrying about that missed deadline and your lover who won't call. Still not convinced? Here's a few more reasons:

It's empowering.

You see something you like. Something that makes you smile. Something that lights up something somewhere near your chest area, your brain area, or maybe even your loins. You have either some money in the bank, your pockets, or on a credit card. You make an executive decision to use that money to buy that thing that makes you smile. And BAM, you own it. Just like that. You get to take it home and put it up any damn place you like.

Artists could use the cash.

Seriously. Artists live by the mantra of not just finding beauty but creating it. And they generally make less money than school teachers. Sometimes a lot less. If you want the world to be better, it starts with finding beauty, and it flows from there to helping its creator pay the rent.

Support what you love.

There are many things to be upset about, many things to rail against, to protest, and to fight. And many of those fights are noble. And it is a far more powerful act to find out what you love and support it. That is the best way I know to make the world a better place.

It's an affirmation of abundance.

When you buy art, you're telling the universe a thing or two. Including that you are confident of your place in it, and that you are worthy of its beauty. You are casting a vote for what's important. And you are doing something to counter the message of the mass-produced goods culture that surrounds you.

It has a story.

I don't know about you, but I want the things I have to have a story. Not to be cold, machine-produced duplicates. To have a life of their own. We all have stories to tell. Countless stories, in truth. And that's exactly what art does. No matter what kind of art it is. It tells stories.

What comes around goes around.

When you start focusing on beauty. When you invest in it, feed it, and nurture it. Then something magical starts to happen. It brings its friends. And more and more beauty just starts showing up at your door, in your car, on a walk, or at work. Maybe even in bed. So go ahead. Buy some art. You'll be happy. And the world will be happier, too.

27

BELIEVE IN ART

We are allowed to grieve, even for things not right for us. The wrong career path, the faithless lover, the secure job that doesn't feed us, the accidentally deleted chapter, the abusive parent, the lottery ticket that blew away.

We are allowed to grieve our youthful recklessness, our wavering self-confidence, our blissful ignorance, our will to live. In other words, we are allowed to be human.

A while back I turned down the job offer of a lifetime. A position in that would provide two paychecks a month, health benefits, and retirement, for something I'm already skilled and experienced in doing.

Why would any reasonable, rational person do this? The answer is that no person in that frame of mind would. But that doesn't mean I didn't have good reasons. Not the least of which is: I need to write. It is that simple.

Follow your bliss and the universe will open doors for you where there were only walls.

So said Joseph Campbell. How many of us truly believe in this? How many act upon that belief? Do I believe? On good days. Do I act on that belief? Well, in that case I did. In truth, I have been for years. Every time I put words to paper. So far though, most of those doors I've had to kick down or pry open.

I'm not whining. Ok, I'm whining a little. I understand that most writers work in the dark, with mostly self-manufactured hope. Which is known to wane from time to time. Unless you are one of those blissfully self-confident types. Which probably means you're not a writer. So forget that last part.

As a writer, I believe in a few irrational things. One is that I can make a decent living as an artist. Despite society's reluctance to do things like fund the arts or pay for books and music, I believe we still live in a world where the gift of art is essential to our lives.

Also, I still I grieve. For the opportunity I passed up, for the simplicity and stability it would have offered. And I also know myself well enough to understand that I am simply unable to cut the rope on all my head-banging-against-walls aspirations. On the writer's shack in my backyard. On becoming living proof of the ability to live our dreams.

We cannot see into the future to determine what will be, what would have been. We cannot see into past lives to recapture what we learned there. Even looking backwards into this life, we are unable see clearly. Our vision is clouded by the lens of perception. Blake said, *If the doors of perception were cleansed everything would appear to man as it is, Infinite.* But absent the aid of mescaline or DMT, this is a difficult state to achieve.

What are we to do then, those of us so unavoidably fixed in our artistic inclinations? I see plenty of ridiculously talented artists around. Those who work the scene constantly, are connected and knowledgeable, and still must bartend or pull espresso in order to pay their rents.

There must be a way to rebuild our communities, our society, our nation-state, our world, so the bankers and defense contractors have to bus tables on the side. And the artists of the world, who enrich our lives so much more, could just focus on their art.

True, it isn't just about money. Money, though, is an undeniable fact of life. Money is energy, a spirit made flesh. Like air or food, we rely upon it for our existence. If we had a thought to completely eschew money, we wouldn't have incarnated here. We'd have stayed in the unbroken realm of light.

Because we are here, we agreed at some point to take on this messy state of being. We agreed to ride the ever-shifting balance between the mud and the rays of light. Wearing this skin means we not only experience joy and happiness, but doubt, grief, and sorrow. One of the tricks to being human is to master the alchemy of turning these states of being into beauty.

If we want our lives to be filled with beauty, we must be brave enough to create it, generous enough to pay for it, compassionate enough to support it, and bold enough to see our vision through to fruition.

> *When you want something, all the universe*
> *conspires in helping you to achieve it.*
> —Paulo Coelho

Despite my occasional frustration, I still believe. And I still grieve. And this is the clay from which art is made.

28

STORIED LIFE

Your life becomes the shape of the days you inhabit.
−John O'Donohue

To a Foodie, you are what you eat. Buddhists say you are what you think. And for Fashionistas, you are what you wear. To me, you are the stories you tell. The stories you watch, the stories you read, the stories you live.

If this is true, then if I watch too many movies, or read too many books, or if I'm too involved with pop culture, will I lose touch with reality? Put another way, will I create a false reality, one that's not really mine? I know people who live in these fantasy worlds, where they are more involved in the lives of imaginary characters than in their own. Living other people's lives instead of theirs.

One's real life is often the life that one does not lead.
−Oscar Wilde

These questions lead to another: *What is reality, anyway?* I remind myself of the importance of myth. I remember the vital purpose of imagination. And I resolve that the retelling of human stories is essential to our humanness.

Before there were movies and books, there were stories. Usually told by elders around fires, these stories wove together the people and the land, the wind and the sun, the animals and the rain. The stories were their lives, just as the rivers were their blood. There was no separation.

In modern life, most of our storytelling is done through movies and books (also television, theatre, opera, video games, and urban legends). Though any stories that people tell, however they tell them—on video, paper, canvas, or clay—they all tell us something, not just about the subjects they depict, but about ourselves.

Where our lives begin and the stories end is perhaps not so important. Because the stories are really pieces of us. Reflections. Living metaphors. By allowing these stories to blur the edges of reality a little, we may come to see ourselves more clearly.

> *When having a smackerel of something with a friend,*
> *don't eat so much that you get stuck*
> *in the doorway trying to get out.*
> –Winnie the Pooh

Stories—and the myths they represent—are great, that is to say, until we get stuck in one. Like good books, we are meant to finish one and pick up the next. Not to read the same chapter, page, sentence over and over.

One way to break out of a story is to go see something of the rest of world. A long time ago, in a galaxy far, far away, I took a months-long backpacking trip through India. I was stuck reading the same story and decided there were no books in my part of the world that could tell me anything new. So I took off in search of buried treasure in the East, to a place where ancient treasure is reported to be hidden. I put aside television, movies, and everything I thought I knew about myself and my place in the world and just went in search of a new story.

It was transformational in ways I may never fully digest. I did find treasure there, though not quite the ones I set out to find. Among the stories which India told me was the one where I needed to go to India to figure out that I didn't need to go to India. And I couldn't have known that any other way. Because familiarity blinds us to these kind of simple truths.

There are billions of universes inside every one of us. We carry them in our blood, our breath, our DNA. And in those universes, every particle of every star, every atom of every moon, each drop of water, has its own history to uncover, its own path to travel, its own story to tell. Each one unique. Each one waiting to be discovered.

But you have to know how to listen, and you have to know how to look. You have to put down that same book you've been reading, turn off the reruns, mix up some new paints. You have to pull out some fresh paper and pick up a new pen.

Let me know what you find. I love a good story.

29

NOTES ON MADNESS & ART

LET'S TALK ABOUT THE PERCEPTIBLY IMPOSSIBLE task of juggling life with art. The elusive balance between art on one side of the equation. And family. And money. And other jobs. And difficult kids. And countless pulls and tugs of meetings and school and bills and doctors and oil changes and shopping for health insurance and pulling weeds and cleaning the garage and shopping for clean food and paying attention to the cyclone of disastrous political shenanigans and the daily researching of a hundred different things for as many reasons.

Of course, there's also the sway of whiskey. Which sometimes brings gold but more often is just a waste of time and calories. And then there's sex and what it is and what it could be and what it should be and when it will come again and whether you did all the things you should before during and after it. There's also the finding time (and energy) for it.

Still there are innumerable other unreasonable demands on your time and energy. And maybe I shouldn't even mention sleep and vacations. These and other superhuman tasks we are just supposed to figure out.

To make good art requires us to know and feel our emotions. To bear our souls while we also bare them. To be vulnerable enough to lay our hearts out on the table for the world to see. And then be strong enough to remain standing if they are judged too harshly.

We are charged with this work and more. Like holding the light with one hand, while stitching the world together with the other. We must be shape-shifters. We must walk in multiple worlds, serve as ambassadors to each one, remember the different languages and customs here and there, and not completely crack the fuck up.

If we succeed, we are gods. If not, we're dreamers and castoffs. Fledgling humans who couldn't make it in the world where the grown-ups live. We must simultaneously love the world and also know when to tell it to fuck-off. So we can do our work. We must resist being thrown off kilter by the siren call of mediocrity. We must question everything and still have the confidence to follow our own voices, to be focused enough not lose them in the crowd.

As you probably know, the pull of the crowd is strong. I don't just mean wanting to fit in or be liked. I mean the ever-rushing current of the modern world. I'm not saying I have definitive answers to any of these riddles. My best advice is to do like Same Phillips says and no matter what happens, *hold on to your voice.*

30

CREATE IT

You will never live if you are looking for the meaning of life.
—Albert Camus

I KNOW WHAT YOU'RE DOING. You're out there turning over stones in search of some deeper meaning to your existence. And when you do, you're going to find some things: moss, algae, bugs, discarded exoskeletons. Your toes are going to sink into the mud. And you're going to get wet. You're going to feel the stream's current on your calves. And you'll probably discover some other hidden treasures you never expected.

What you will not find are any engraved explanations, no statements of empirical meaning, no one-size-fits-all answers. That's because life is not some big game of hide and seek, where the gods have written down the correct answers under certain stones, and the only game is for you to look in the right places. Though, come to think of it, that would make a good story.

Let me be clear, I do believe in living a life filled with turning over stones. And if you enjoy playing in rivers and creeks, hunting fairies, and searching for mayflies, then you should continue to do just that. There are treasures to be found everywhere. But just as the beauty beheld depends upon the eyes that seek it out, your life's meaning lies in the joys of your own experience.

Do we find meaning or does it find us?

Let me say that another way. The meaning of life is not hiding out there somewhere, waiting to be found. Life has whatever meaning we attach to it. Whatever meaning we imagine for ourselves.

More simply, we do not find meaning; we create it. And when we stop creating meaning, we quickly get lost. And then, though we are in search of meaning, somehow we end up looking for ourselves. And we don't realize that now we are two steps away from the answer.

And when we begin to feel better, it isn't because we have found ourselves, or our way home, or even discovered the elusive meaning we sought. It is because we have assigned some meaning to our present experience. Randomly or not. Of our own design or someone else's.

What does it mean to *mean*?

What does it mean for something to have meaning? How do we know when anything is meaningful? Too often, we believe it is when another person, religion, institution, television show, or cereal box tells us it does. But this adopted meaning often doesn't ring true.

Meanings are a lot like fingerprints. Consider a rose. To a photographer, the meaning of the rose is its vibrant color. To a sculptor, its texture. To the blind, its smell. To a lover, its symbol of affection. To a gardener, its reflection of success.

To a bee, the sustenance it provides. These are each true and meaningful aspects of a rose. And yet, no one could ever say that any of these was the one true meaning of a rose. It is also why it cannot be said that anything is inherently meaningless.

You can do this with almost anything. Take a songbird. I may see waking up to bird songs at dawn as the Universe giving me the best gift it can imagine to start my day. You may grab a pillow and wonder why in the world you've been cursed by the gods. When the gelato café moves in next door to your workplace, you may celebrate it as proof that you are, in fact, the chosen one of the goddess. Where your best friend may view it as yet another obstacle to a happy bikini season.

What do you mean by *create?*

Isn't that like making it up? Are you saying we are just making up things about life so we'll feel better? Well, yes, in a way. But more than that, I'm saying that the meaning of life is not set. It is not some fixed, static thing. Otherwise you could just look it up in the dictionary and move on.

We live in an interactive universe. The meaning of anything in life is not separate from you. We all create our lives and their meaning. Everyday. All day long. Life is not a board game and we are not game pieces.

When a painter paints a picture, everyone agrees that the painter has created something. But the act of creation is not limited to art. It is spread across all aspects of our lives. Your life's meaning is no different. You are constantly deciding what is meaningful.

Consciously create.

We are unconscious of most of the assignments of meaning in our lives. Often because we've mindlessly adopted someone else's decisions. But we can change that. We can be mindful of the unique fingerprints of our own world of meaning. We can do it in a way that keeps us awake. And we can do that moment by moment.

I think what Camus meant was to get out of your head. Because the meaning of life is not there. It's in your life. Live your life fully and find your own meanings in the living.

VI

LOVE & OTHER MISADVENTURES

31

LOVE

I MEAN THAT NOT AS A NOUN, not even as a verb, but as a command. Or, more poignantly, as a simple instruction for life. As a game plan with only one play. A game plan that should be tattooed, not taped, to your wrist.

Love is simple.

We confuse and distract ourselves with hundreds of strategies for happiness, for success, for control, for security, for life. When the answer is simple. Albeit, counter-intuitive. In our defense, this is probably because, while this one-word-directive may seem simple, somehow it is not.

The reasons why are probably fodder for at least twelve months of essays, all by themselves. But I think it is mostly because we are fearful beings. No matter what we say or how we act.

Love is dangerous.

No matter the bravado. No matter the hours at the gym, the tattoos, the sexy clothes, the cadre of friends, the cool job, or the hipness of our hangouts.

No matter the number of times we read these words, study them in books, pay teachers to tell us, repeat them in mantras, stack the pillows, clear our minds, burn the right incense. No matter our friend counts, the notches on the bedpost or the numbers in the bank. No matter our previous revelations.

Love remembers.

We forget. We lose faith. We doubt. We disbelieve. We call past successes flukes and focus only on failure. We begin again our strategies for survival. Yes, survival. We decide that all else is fool-hearted frivolity. That we need to spend less time watching the stars and more time watching our backs.

We fall back into fear. Because fear is easy. Fear comforts us as it tell us lies. Fear gets our back, it says. Protects our hearts, it assures. Leads us not into temptation. Not to cliffs and falls. Fear teaches us lessons in letting ourselves be too free. Lest we forget again. Lest we let our hearts hold the reins again. Lest we lose our way. Again.

Love knows the truth.

And the truth is not easy. The truth is not simple. Not courteous or kind. The truth is blinding in its beatitudes. Ruthless in its revelations. And above all, breathtaking in its beauty. And beauty, well, you know what that is.

Love is beauty.

In all its shapes and sizes. In all its gifts and grandeur. In its bliss and its barely believableness. In its understatement and its overwhelm. In its cruelty and its crystalline clarity. In its ability to break your heart and to save your life. With one swift stroke.

Yes, it is true. The answer is simple. It is taking our own advice that is hard. Even as I write this, I must remind myself that it is true. Because I'm no different from you. And you're no different from her or him. Which leads us back to the reason there is only one rule.

Love is everywhere.

Yes, I mean literally everywhere. As in not figuratively. As in you need only reach out and your fingers will touch it. As in take a step forward and you can't help but bump into it. As in open your mouth and some of it will come out. As in open your heart and some of it can't help but spill inside.

And so why aren't we all just constantly swimming around in blissful revelations of beauty and self-awareness and fulfillment? Well, because.

Love is complicated.

Or as I've said, *love breaks all rules / ignores all customs / cuts through fences / slips across front lines / trespasses against us / steals what it pleases / pleases its victims / slays its critics / bleeds us to delirium / and saves our souls. No matter the cost.* (from *love: study 1, Waking Up at Rembrandt's*)

Sometimes this simple directive to love is hard to follow, sometimes it's easy. But whatever action you take, if you do it with your heart open, that is enough. That will change the results. It will change your reaction. And it will change your experience. Of yourself. Of others. Of your whole damn life.

Love takes many shapes.

Love is not being foolish or naive, not shirking from who you are, not being afraid to use your voice. Love is showing up, reaching out, standing in your gifts, sharing your vision, connecting, being open. And as you probably already know, doing these things is both wonderful and terrifying.

In the end, there is only love. Because in the beginning there is only love. So giving the instruction is simple. And yes, acting on it takes a little more. A little more courage. A little more faith. A little better memory. A little thicker skin. But in the end, what is required is the willingness to let love have its way with you. Or as Mr. Kravitz so artfully taught us:

Let love rule.

32

WHAT IS LOVE?

NEVER HAS THERE BEEN A WORD more filled with promise than this one. With just four letters, the word conjures up the noblest of thoughts, the richest of emotions, and the surest guarantees of fulfillment. The very sight of the word has the power to send even the most cynical of us to our knees. And yet, do we even know what it means?

I'm told that Sanskrit has 96 different words for love. I don't read or write Sanskrit, so I can't swear by that. But a guy named Robert Johnson said so. Not the Robert Johnson you're thinking of, the blues man, though that would be cool, too. The Robert Johnson who was a student of Krishnamurti—who probably actually knew Sanskrit.

But what is the point of having 96 words for something when you really only need one? Well, I think the point is that whenever anyone uses one of the 96 words in Sanskrit— everyone else knows exactly what kind of love they're talking about. The rest of us English speakers, not so much.

If I say *I love you* to any of you, what does that mean? I can say it to my child, my partner, my pets, my mom, my friends. I can also say it about a painting, a sunset, a car, a phone, or a beer. Does it all mean the same thing? I can love the color blue.

I can love a post on Facebook. I can love a movie. And I can love the face you just made.

We could say there were categories for the English word love, like romantic love, familial love, and friendship love. But these aren't really adequate. Because the love of one's child is quite different from the love of one's siblings, or even the love of parents. And we don't love all our friends the same.

There are definitely many kinds of romantic love. Everything from infatuation, to the kind that takes your breath away, to that which has survived years of marriage, kids, joy, and loss. And of course, there is that blurry line between love and lust. Who among us has mastered the ability to always tell them apart?

There are even the ones we love though they cause us more pain than joy. Because anyone who has been there knows that even the best loves come with healthy doses of pain. As Sting wisely observed, *Love is the child of an endless war.*

Let's say we're just going to talk about romantic love. And just the variety of romantic love that is accompanied by racing hearts and sweaty palms. Of all the billions of stories told since the beginning of the human experiment, none is more common than this one. And yet every time we tell it to ourselves it feels brand new. Made just for us. And we're sure that there's never been another person who has ever felt this way. And maybe we're right. Which means there are billions of individual romantic loves that all share nearly the same DNA, but are still as distinguishable as snowflakes and fingerprints.

There are those people who have really only had one romantic love their whole lives. But for most of us there have been more than that. And each of them has been different, even though we've used the same word to describe them all. The Beatles said that *love is all you need*. If love is that big, then how can one word be sufficient?

Why, with all of our creativity and ingenuity, have we not split the word into its potentially infinite parts. How can it be that we can split an atom but not a word? Especially a word as important as this.

Let's not stop there. Let's consider that we don't even know what kind of word we're talking about. Is it a noun or a verb? Is love something tangible that we can hold in our hands? Is it an action, something that we must do or that must be done to us? Or a feeling that arrives at our doorstep from lands unknown. And then disappears into the night.

Maybe love isn't something that preexists at all, but something we build. Or maybe it's the material we build with. Maybe it isn't a thing at all, but a place we inhabit. Maybe it's a way of seeing the world. Even a way of being in the world. Maybe it's none of these. Or maybe it's all of them. Sheryl Crowe said *love is all there is*. And I know a Medicine Woman who teaches the same thing, that everything is love, including fear and hate.

If there is nothing that is not love, then we have really, truly done it a disservice with our woefully inadequate one-word label. Or maybe not. Maybe love is too big to be contained in words. And so the best we can do is to come up with as simple a word as possible to point to a thing that is beyond all things.

33

LONELY HEARTS CLUB

> *Millions of people in this world, all of them yearning,*
> *looking to others to satisfy them,*
> *yet isolating themselves.*
> – Haruki Murakami

IT MAY OR MAY NOT BE FEBRUARY when you read this. But all of us can remember the annual season of Valentine's hearts wherever we look. You've likely added to the fortune of Victoria's Secret as they capitalize on our hormonally infused aspirations of coital bliss. You may have also been part of the non-coupled population who is alone and often deeply resentful of all the hoopla.

I've been alone on the 14th before, drinking wine, listening to Cowboy Junkies, and wondering, "Yeah, *where are you tonight?*" I've been a part of singles-night rebellions to the annual couples-fest, where I've hit the town with others of my lot and pretended we didn't care. But we each still went home alone at the end of the night. And if any of us were honest, there was something about it that stung.

> *Maybe ever'body in the whole damn world*
> *is scared of each other.*
> –John Steinbeck

This is not to equate being alone with loneliness. The two are definitely not the same. One can be lonely in a crowd of people, even familiar people. The kind of lonely we experience with our families, our boyfriends, girlfriends, and spouses is the most poignant of all.

Any adequate discussion of the origin of this loneliness would be far too large to fit in this space. But there can be no question that loneliness is a word that lies near the core of our human troubles. It is also (ironically) true that our fear of one another creates a chasm that is difficult to bridge.

> *I want to be with those*
> *who know secret things or else alone.*
> –Ranier Maria Rilke

One thing seems certain, if we are to survive, we must address this loneliness conundrum. We need to create communities filled with people who are not afraid of each other. A world where we no longer feel the need to lock our doors and sleep with guns under our pillows.

We need to dust off our natural curiosity about the world and the people in it, instead of hiding behind ignorance and misunderstanding. And we need to figure out how to see ourselves as more alike than different.

> *Loneliness is the human condition.*
> *Cultivate it. The way it tunnels into you*
> *allows your soul room to grow.*
> *—Janet Fitch*

We must learn to see our own reflections in the faces of the happy couples around us. And we need to accept the importance of cultivating solitude.

Maybe if we can be okay with ourselves, we can enjoy being by ourselves, as well as with others. Maybe if we can be okay with ourselves, we won't always need to be part of a couple. Or maybe if we can be okay with ourselves, we will attract others who are okay with themselves. And then none of us will need to be alone.

> *Loneliness is the unloneliest feeling in the world,*
> *as everyone has experienced it.*
> *—Jarod Kintz*

So if you find yourself single on Valentine's Day or any other day, there are all kinds of ways to not be by yourself. The main thing to know is that if you are feeling lonely, you're not alone.

34

THE HEART OF EWE

i am the lion and
you are the lamb and
as prophesied,
we will lie down together.

because love is greater
than the sum of its parts.

—from *love: study 1*
Waking Up at Rembrandt's

THE SKY TELLS ITS OWN STORIES. Like the one written down in the English proverb where March comes in like a lion and then leaves like a lamb. If you watch the night sky, the constellation Leo rises in late February and by April's dawn, Aries has taken its place.

Though the stars foretell this story of growth, of self-awareness, of maturing and finding peace, it doesn't always happen. In fact, it doesn't happen that often.

Most people do not find peace. We come into the world with a roar. Screaming our names to the sky. Pissed off about the bumpy flight. Unhappy we had to leave our warm and cozy wombs. We scream and cry throughout early childhood, often for no apparent reason. By age two, the ego has come onto center stage, doing what the ego does best: *want*. Perpetually want, no matter how many wants are met, never being satisfied.

In most cases, this behavior does not stop with toddlerhood. Though we grow into adult-sized bodies, take on adult-sized tasks, pay adult-sized bills, feed and dress ourselves, we are still prone to the same tantrums. Sometimes we throw these tantrums where others can see; most often they rage on inside us.

The wars we've become hopelessly addicted to in the world at large actually rage inside each one of us. The corporate world's destructive greed comes from our own insatiable hunger. The anger and hatred we show one another comes from the lion's roar inside each of us. From an animal inside us who—despite the years, the clothes, the utensils, and the words it has learned—has blindly refused to evolve. Or maybe it simply forgot it was supposed to.

Maybe it stopped looking up at the sky for guidance. It stopped reading the stories of the lions who went before it. It closed its eyes to beauty. It came to believe the lie that survival depends upon burying the heart. When the opposite is actually true.

> *Fear an ignorant man more than a lion.*
> –Turkish proverb

The lamb knows the simple answer that eludes many searching lions: Letting go is the secret to everything. Letting go is understanding that this moment is enough. In this, the lamb loves more fiercely than any lost lion can imagine. In this, the lamb is the lionhearted.

Go ahead, roar like a lamb.

35

WTAF

THIS IS WHAT VIRTUALLY EVERYONE I have ever known has said about love at one time or another in their lives. Well, maybe not those exact words, but you know. Because really, let's face it, love is a m!#&*!f#$!*r.

I know, I know, I have written over and over about the wonder and beauty of love. About how all we need is love, because love is all there is. I have echoed Bryan Ferry and agreed that *there is nothing / more than this.*

And I meant all of those things. Really.

It's just that there is this other side of love. And it's kind of dark. Sometimes it's black as the coal you wish your ex-lover had gotten from Santa.

Sometimes it can feel so dark it seems there's no way any light will ever escape from it again. But then, some poor fool lights a candle of hope somewhere down the corridor and you decide you'd better get up and go check it out.

Too many metaphors?

The point is, here's this thing that totally baffles us, shatters us, leaves us inoperable, unsure, raw. And yet we can't help but bend to its call, its command, its seduction.

So, back to the question of *wtaf*? I don't mean to mislead you here. I don't actually have an answer to the question. And besides, what is there to say about love that hasn't already been inked.

But then again, if love is all there is, all there is actually is quite a lot. So there has to be more to say.

Quoting an ancient poet, Shawn Colvin sang us a cautionary tale of the 84,000 different delusions. I used to think this was a reference to the number of seconds there are in a day. Until I learned that there are 86,400 seconds in a day. For the sake of poetry, let's say there's 84,000. Anyway, something like 83,000 of the delusions must have to do with love. (The others are probably things like time, impermanence, and those wavy lines that look like water on the horizon when it's really hot.) Because love is not something we define. Love is something that defines us.

And for most of us, that is terrifying.

Because we want to be mysterious. Mysterious is interesting. Mysterious is seductive. Mysterious keeps us safe.

Mysterious does not allow us to wander the dark alleys of love, nor trespass on the grounds of lust, nor attempt to swim in the murky waters of infatuation. Wait, that is exactly what mysterious entices us to do. It can do all this because uncertainty is exhilarating.

Who wants to be safe, when we can be alive?

Even if we are absolutely tortured by love, it has a way of placing us right in the center of our humanness. And that is where we get to find out who we are.

Back on the subject of things left to say about love, I can say this: At this time in our evolution as a species, it seems critically important to choose love. Not that it is possible to choose anything but love, really, if you accept the premise that love is all there is. Damn, I did it again. I opened Pandora's box and another paradox slipped out into the universe.

The truth is the simple (or not-so-simple) act of choosing love is an infinitely powerful one. If you don't believe me, just think about any time in your life when you've done it. Chosen love, that is. Intoxicating, right? Worth all the trouble. And I'm not just talking about romance. Any act of love, no matter how small, fills us with the elixir of life.

Maybe I was hiding an answer to the question after all. If there is one, it is this: We keep choosing love because love is the best game in town. When we choose love, we choose life. And life, with all its doubt, frustration, heartbreak, beauty, ecstasy, and sun-drenched joy is worth all the risk. It's as simple as that.

36

MORE THAN THIS

Do not seek the because—in love there is no because,
no reason, no explanation, no solutions.
    —Anais Nin

IF YOU ARE STILL READING, then you must doubt something of what she is saying. You must believe there is not only a why, but a how. You must have personified love with all the frailness of human understanding. Love is more than this.

We all struggle to know its secret inner workings.

Nevertheless, love simply is. With all due depth and clarity, love simply is. The ultimate answer to the infinite mystery is that love simply is. And what this means is beyond human understanding. Except in those small glimpses we each get. Those times when, voluntarily or not, we meet life up close and with all our fullness. Then we know love, in all its beauty and terror.

When this simple idea (that love is) is not enough for us, when we strive to dissect it further, to name it, label it, categorize it, these are the causes of much suffering. Despite what all the ascended masters tell us, despite what we say in our best hours, despite what your guru teaches and even what Bryan Ferry sings, we believe love is more than this. But what more can there be than what is?

This conundrum, this insatiable need for something more than everything takes up most of human existence. This irrational need turns the conversation toward something that distracts us from the real, the primary, the immediate, the sensual flooding of the spiritual gates.

I suppose it is this mystery within a mystery that leads us to think love can be planned, calendared, defined, or plotted on a graph by human hearts and minds. Trust me, this could never be—though I doubt we will ever stop trying. And that, too, is part of love's gift.

> *All my life, my heart has yearned*
> *for a thing I cannot name.*
> –Andre Breton

Love is not subject to our unwittingly small designs, our persistent needs for order, for instant gratification, our stubborn insistence on going in the wrong direction, our misdirected desires, our dearest fears. Love's sight is longer than you may see in a thousand lifetimes. Its wisdom is deeper than a thousand voyages into space. Its compassion is fuller than all the water balloons of all the childhoods of history's memory.

Love is by design. Despite your mistaken beliefs in its timing, its accuracy, its best intentions. Like petals from a faded rose, you must learn to let all these things go. Sit back and be still. Love knows the way.

Next time you think, *oh, that one was such a mistake,* know that you're wrong. Love doesn't make mistakes. Love's intelligence is infinite.

Love is always in alignment. Love is always in synch. Love is always on its game and in the flow. Unlike you and I, love does not need to trip, to stumble, to fall, in order to learn about cracks in the sidewalk, balance, gravity. Love is gravity. Love is the crack in the sidewalk.

> *I think there is no unreturn'd love,*
> *the pay is certain one way or another.*
> –Walt Whitman

VII

LONGING &
Belonging

37

YOU BELONG HERE

WE ALL WANT TO BELONG. It's one of the most fundamental human needs. To connect. To fit in. To be a part of something. Through most of human history, this belonging has meant being part of a people, a culture. Whether we were Irish or Italian or Indian, we inherited ideas about who we were and where we belonged in the world.

Belonging also meant being a part of a landscape and having a well-defined sense of place. The Irish could not parse themselves from their rock walls, their peat fires, or their lush green environments any more than the Native Americans could separate themselves from the rivers, the forests, or the buffalo. These things were part of them, every bit as much as the blood in their veins, the air in their lungs.

But things have changed. To travel any appreciable distance from one's home was once considered an epic adventure. Today, technological advances have allowed us not only to travel to remote parts of the world, but to do it easily and often. Our work may relocate us several times in our lives, often to other countries.

While we have gained much with this mobility, we have also lost much. Including our innate sense of place. To be sure, there are positive aspects to this. Like the disappearance of cultural barriers. But our cultural identities are not easily divisible from our natural environment, and along the way we've unwittingly sacrificed the innate sense of stewardship that comes with being culturally connected to the land.

I was not born in the Sierras. And yet, they have become enmeshed in my identity. Just as Lake Tahoe, the Truckee River, and Pyramid Lake have become part of me. But fewer and fewer people share this kind of attachment to places these days. Somehow, our mobile society has abandoned its ability—or at least its tendency—to put down roots, in favor of a non-committal relationship with our environments.

In defense of modern technology, I confess there are other reasons for the disconnect. Cultural anthropologists tell us that this phenomenon did not begin with trains or cars or airplanes, but with the written word itself. That's right, ironically, writing shares some of the blame. In oral cultures, studies show, there is a seamless connection between a tree, the spoken sound for tree, and the relationship of the people to the trees.

Once we remove ourselves one step from the tree by creating a written word to refer to the tree, the disconnect begins. Before we know it, we are polluting the rivers and the land and not understanding what dumping waste into the ocean could possibly have to do with us. We forget the lessons of Camelot that the king and the land are one. This may seem like hyperbole. It is not.

There are other factors, of course, televisions, iPads, and air conditioning, to name a few. When was the last time you took a book out in your backyard to read? When was the last time you went barefoot in the grass or went for a walk along the river? When did you just sit on a rock and look at the mountains? Without your phone.

A short time ago—in recent memory—we were not so leashed to the imaginary world playing out on our smartphones that we couldn't have a conversation over dinner. Sadly, our Facebook pages are now the kinds of things that hold a sense of place for many of us.

It doesn't have to be this way. Though it is a slightly warmer place than it used to be, the real world still exists. And so do the people in it. Otherwise known as your community. And I do not mean your social media followers. I mean those that live in the physical world with you. Those who share the same water, rocks, and air.

This is a big conversation. And I've only just dipped my toe in in the water here. I'm going to wade a little deeper into the river and turn over some more rocks. In the meantime, I want you to do the same. After all, in this conversation, as in countless other ways, we belong together.

38

GIVE IT UP

I CANNOT READ POETRY. I don't know when it happened. But I noticed it today. I turned to a page filled with delicate memories of a childhood. Of tooth fairies and pixie dust footprints. And found my skin so raw, my tears so close, my throat so narrow, that I couldn't read on. I just put it down.

What is it in us that urges us not to feel. Why is sadness so seductive and so painful. Why is art so deft at finding that tender spot. At striking so straight and true at its target.

Why are words so powerful. After all this time. Why aren't we more immune to their effect, their seduction.

And why, despite this power that words wield, do I sometimes think about quitting. You know, just turning them off. And not just the words, but the voices that carry them. The ears that hear them. The mouth that whispers their names. The desire to pin more of them to a page.

As if they were exotic butterflies. And I were some kind of *ento-etymologist* studying their behavior, their migration patterns, their mating rituals. Their distinguishing marks. Maybe it's because chasing butterflies is hard work.

The truth is we all need a break from even the best parts of ourselves from time to time. And from the ambitious hopes that carrot us along most days.

None of us are strangers to the crushing waves of doubt that pound our shores. Or to the trip wires we must avoid as we run the chase-your-dreams marathon towards the lives we aspire to live. And there are those moments where the chase just seems to have gone out of our legs.

There are days where we all just need someone to say: Go ahead. Give up. You can, you know. After all, always living for a dream somewhere out the in the future is an impediment to actually living right here.

We want an alternate reality. Somewhere we have permission to take a long nap in a world without alarm clocks. A spa day that lasts for weeks. A foot massage that brings us enlightenment.

Or maybe we just need a place to be free. Because most of us are slaves to something. Money. Our jobs. Television. The internet. Our minds. Dogma. Our possessions. Half-understood beliefs. Obsessions. Escapisms. Fear. Ignorance. Prejudice. Doubt.

Maybe we need to live in a world where we matter, without regard to resume entries, social media, or sales quotas. Where we can forget things like tweets, relevance, likes, and friend requests.

Maybe to be free is to have found our home. Our passion. Our voice. Our tribe. And our ability to be our authentic selves.

Maybe it's a place where we own our days, our time, our direction. Where we choose where to pour our passions and when. Without having to lug around that oversized dollar sign all day. The one that doesn't quite fit on my writing desk.

The one that's hard to pack around on a spontaneous hike in the foothills. That acts as a roadblock to countless creative projects. That comes with its own defeatist recordings that play on loop.

Or maybe we just need to be free to follow our voices. To understand, in every cell of our bodies, that now is all we have. That we no longer need to carry the weight of the future. We never did. We can just let it fall to the ground. Right here. Because someday is imaginary.

This is my prayer. For me and for you.

That we find this place to go. This place to belong. Where we use our voices. Where they are heard. And where we do not waste this wild and precious life just paying rent.

To find that place, we may need to learn something new. Like how to let go of more. Because sometimes all we need is nothing. Just space and silence. Maybe the next time we reach for answers and come up empty, we can begin to understand that empty is the best thing to be.

It's worth a try. Turn down the noise. Turn off the screen. Unplug your thoughts. Just be free. Try to remember what that even is. Forget that life is short. Remember you are infinite. Right where you are.

39

WE'RE ALL OUTSIDERS

You're cruising social media and watching the daily unfolding of other people's lives. Not very many years ago this was called stalking, or maybe worse if you were looking in the windows of someone's house. But now the windows of others' lives are flung open wide. And we've all become voyeurs.

That is to say, outsiders looking in.

When I say all of us, it is true. Because there's an opportunity cost to everything. If you're doing this, you're not doing that. If you're out and about with friends, you're not in and cozy with someone you love. If you're working on an exciting and ambitious project, you're not on the beach somewhere.

Fear of missing out is not really all that new. It's just enhanced by our technologically-centered lives. We are addicted to our phones because they have become our replacement connection to the world and the people around us.

I use the word addiction, because that's what it is.

One of my favorite books as a kid was *The Outsiders*, by S.E. Hinton. Kind of a *West Side Story* set in the Midwest. A rich kid-poor kid thing, where the heroes were all poor kids.

I guess I've always liked the underdogs.

I don't think I really got the title back then. I liked the characters. I liked their odd names. And though I didn't go to a private school, or have a lot of money, my life still had almost nothing in common with the lives of the Northside *greasers*. Still, I related to them and to their palpable but unspoken desire to be connected somehow to the world around them. Even though that same world had cast them to the margins. Or maybe because of it.

We all need to belong. It is essential.

Some stories never really leave us. And while our need to connect likely has its roots in something deeply biological, like safety and survival, it has evolved over time to something much greater. New research shows that addiction has a lot to do with a lack of connection to other humans.

The new science shows we actually require social connection in order for our brains to develop properly, to continue to operate properly. But if we somehow skipped that step, science also shows it is possible for our short-circuited brains to rewire themselves. With every external connection we make, whether through touch, eye contact, talking, listening, or laughter, we create new neural pathways. These external connections allow us to create new internal connections.

In other words, as inside, so outside.

And speaking of outside. Spending time in nature also rewires our brains. In our increasingly urbanized lives, it's actually mandatory for us to spend more time in nature in order to avoid the onset of mental illness. *Mandatory*, think about that.

Who do you know who isn't a little bit off these days?

I'm not just talking about the ionic benefits of being near the ocean. (Although that definitely works.) We need to walk on the Earth's skin, not just our concrete sidewalks. We need to surround ourselves with trees, to walk beside the melodic sound of streams, to touch our bare feet to the grass, to feast upon the bright colored leaves, to crunch them in our hands, beneath our feet, to put our cheeks to the soft furry moss, feel the wind in our faces, and smell the vast fecundity of the natural world.

We need to remember our true home.

And we need to remember that our technological connections, as mind-bendingly instantaneously gratifying as they are, are just metaphors for the real thing. We need to remember not to forget how to have a real conversation, to look each other in the eyes, to give freely of our hugs and smiles, to be genuinely interested in the lives of others. And to not be so focused on the moment-by-moment self-promotion of our own.

Here's your challenge: practice putting down your phone a little more each day. When you feel the tug of that leash, turn instead to one of the humans closest to you. Buy them coffee, give them a hug, or take them on a walk in the trees. Your brain will thank you. And your heart might even start dancing.

40

THE THINGS WE WANT

I'VE BEEN THINKING OF ALL THESE THINGS WE WANT. It starts with all the little things, like a new shirt or nice weather. Then the list quickly grows to include the things we obsessively want. The things we crave like oxygen.

I understand we're biologically hardwired to seek out what we need. From an evolutionary standpoint, this makes sense. Food and sex, for instance. We each must eat so we survive. And we must have sex so our species survives.

But there are other things that aren't so easily explained. Music. Coffee. Intoxicants. Words. Touch. What is even more mysterious is how we've been programmed to feel bad about what we want. As if this could possibly serve any evolutionary purpose.

Some of these things we want to the point of distraction. To the point of self-destruction even. This seems like a design flaw. That we could not only feed our wants to the point of self-elimination, but that we could also die of want. This seems like a set of Woozle tracks worthy of following.

But first I need to back up a little. I may have said it before, but I'm not really from this world. I am a foreigner of sorts who has learned to order coffee, ask for direction, say *hello* and *thank you*. And I sometimes find myself in a day that I'm just trying to get through. That's it. Make it to the point where I'm free to go to bed. And if I didn't have a child to tend to, that time might be really early. Like 10:30. In the morning.

I only mention this because the cousin of *want* is *despair*. You may think that someone who writes mostly feel-good essays is a stranger to despair. But this is far from true. I am intimate with despair. And that is why I can tell you it's okay if you happen to find yourself there.

Go ahead. Wallow a bit. Despair is a necessary rest stop on the road of life. But eventually you must draw a line in the sand, get up, and keep moving. Beyond the occasional cleanse of a good cry, there is little else of lasting value in despair.

There is one other thing, though. When you visit despair, you are required to leave all wants at the door. Despair provides a safe space from all your cravings. Despair empties you of all the things you thought you needed to be whole. It reminds you that, rather than fill you up, all this stuff really just weighs you down.

Despair pulls back the curtain of illusion. It shows you that the glass is neither half full nor half empty. The glass is always full. But half of it is filled with air, with light, with a billion particles of cosmic goo, with stardust. And that stardust is you. You are already there. Already completely whole. Despite despair's best efforts, though, mostly we don't remember this.

Life is fragile, precious, fleeting. We want to drink up as much of it as we can. But our senses can only take us so far. Just ask any addict. Or ask yourself whether food, sex, beer, or Facebook ever really fill you up.

We're a mixture of light and clay. A metaphor of subatomic physics. The more we think of ourselves as only clay, as a pot that can be filled up by any of these things, the more the pot isn't actually there. And you can't hold yesterday's orgasm in a pot that doesn't exist.

Yes, the food tastes great. But it cannot convince you of your self-worth. And your social media feed can spoon you hours of content, but it will never ever leave you sated. And all the likes in the world are not the same thing as one real human moment. One in which you realize that you are not a container at all. You are a Woozle who is hiding just around the next birch tree. And if you are really still, you might even catch yourself.

41

FOLLOW ME

If I knew the way, I would take you home.
−Jerry Garcia

SOCIAL MEDIA has daylighted a number of things about the human condition, aspects of ourselves we previously admitted only in the candlelight of therapy or the confidence of close friends. We are, all of us, more or less desperate for attention. We want to be seen, liked, followed, and shared. By as close to everyone as we can attract, as close to all of the time as possible.

The irony of this newly discovered need to be followed wherever and whenever we go is that, more or less, we are all pretty much lost, pretty much most of the time. Occasionally, we have these moments of clarity. And then, the rest of the time, there's this glimpse, just off to the side, of things we know to be true, of a place of comfort and peace. An oasis of knowing serenity that is familiar, but just not really where we are right now.

Sometimes, the veils of illusion are so thick we lose sight of the oasis altogether. All we know is the general direction where we last spotted it. In these spaces, a wide hole opens up inside us, and despair takes the opportunity to set up its bleak residence there. Despair's opaque nature not only eclipses the oasis, it acts as a blackout curtain to the rest of the world.

Life is ironic.

And sometimes cruel. It seems that the brighter the light someone shines for the rest of the world, the darker it can be in that person's own home. Despair must have sensitive eyes, because when it sets up shop it not only blocks out the sun, it throws blankets over all the lamps inside. And it hangs thick rugs from the ceiling, so the voices from outside can't find their way in.

We are constantly confused when wildly successful and widely beloved people kill themselves. But this is how it happens. All around them, people are following them, liking them, and wanting to be their friend. But they can't see it. Despair is a black hole, devouring all this energy before it can turn into light.

We all need to be seen. And the shortest distance between daylight and despair is this need. Social media feeds the need. And despair has struck an insider's deal, creating an invisible profile everywhere you go. Except it doesn't need to send friend requests. We already follow its hashtag without even knowing it

You are real.

I'd love to tell you that because I know how it happens, I also know the way out. I know how to pull down the rugs and throw off the blankets, open the windows and doors, run out into the rain and the sun and fields. But I'm not sure I do.

The only thing I know is that I've been there. And, like a bad acid trip, somehow I was able to wait it out. That eventually I found myself outside again, staring at the sunrise. Bowing deeply. Breathing in and out. But not everyone is as lucky.

One thing I can do is point out that it's called virtual reality for a reason. It's because it isn't real. But we are real. And we're all in danger of slipping into the matrix. I can remind you that when you are there, and you feel isolated from the whole world, know that you are not actually alone. There are people, things, a world surrounding you, holding you up, wrapping you with blankets, lighting fires, caressing your feet.

The best thing we can do.

The best thing we can do is to talk about it. Reach out to each other. Admit things are not always bright and shiny. You don't have to wallow and roll around in your grief. But learn to turn around and look the monster in the face. Stop running from it. Stop pretending it isn't there.

Believe me when I tell you nobody's life is as good as it looks on social media. When we drag our monsters out into the light, when we use our words to expose them, they lose most of their powers. We see them clearly for what they are: parlor tricks, illusions, games that are rigged.

Our words are bridges to everyone else sitting in the dark right now. Dare to speak up. Have the courage to use your voice. And the compassion to reach out your hand. Light candles for others with your words and remind them there's a way out of the dark.

Teach each other to see again.

It wasn't that long ago. When we lived in a world without smartphones and social media. When the light we craved came from the sun, not the screen. When we connected with each other over coffee, shared stories and smiles over the Sunday Times, and liked the sand under our feet, the grass between our toes. That world is still there. And so are we.

If we can learn to talk about things like despair, we can also teach ourselves to see beyond it. We can train our cat eyes to see in the dark, our ears to hear the faintest of songs. Even if we're not sure of the way home, we can teach each other to look for road markers. And we can remind each other what is real.

We can leave the ropes we've used to find our way, so there will be lifelines for others. We can weave our own real world internet with them. We can light candles where we go, so others can find their way to us. And if some of us lose our light, we can still walk each other home.

42

HOWL

Some people will say I stole that title from beat poet Allen Ginsberg. Though if I did, it wasn't intentional. It's just how it came out. And so I let it. And you should, too. If you want to live, that is.

In any case, nobody owns that word. Or any word. Put another way, we each own every word that comes from our authentic voices. Because those words are what matter. And little else.

I'm not saying words are the only thing that matter. I'm saying your words, from your voice, no matter their shape, are what matter. I'm saying using someone else's words, hiding behind them for safety, illusion, respectability, while understandable, won't move your piece down the board at all. Do not pass Go. Do not collect $200.

More importantly, they won't lead to an understanding of yourself or the world, which is essential to really living. Without your true voice, you'll just be one of the walking dead, another Dr. Malcolm Crowe walking around believing you're alive. (There's a reason why zombie movies are so popular.)

Reach down.

Find what it is that haunts you, moves you, sparks your desire, makes you bleed, won't let you sleep, completely envelops you, tucks you in, and kisses you goodnight. That is what will save you. And most of us need some kind of saving, big or small, from time to time. Maybe forever and always.

I often find myself lost. Somewhere between the world I want to live in and the reality of things like mass poverty, political crimes, profit-based environmental destruction, and sex trade. These worlds are so close to our own, right next door, really. But we all have our own obstacles, which often live much closer, things like equal rights, health insurance, overdue taxes, relationship struggles, and inadequate internet service.

Like you, daily, I have to map my own way out. Towards the ideal creative life of my dreams. Because there is no worn path. No posted signs, no permission slips. There is only my voice. And a long time ago I listened to Sam Phillips when she told me told hold on to it. You should, too.

Find your voice.

If you've made it this far into this piece and you're still wondering what I'm talking about, it's likely because you haven't found it yet. Your thing, your passion, your medicine, your calling, your dream. You know, your voice. (Because we live in the age of YouTube, if you want more of a video example of what I'm talking about, checkout the Power of Words Video Project. www.pow.tlqonline.com)

I'm far from an expert on this sort of thing, but what if there are things more important than enlightenment? Being a whole human being, for instance. I'm not saying that's true. But

I know this one thing, you can't be whole without your voice. Simply impossible. So I think it's safe to say that enlightenment requires wholeness. And wholeness requires a voice.

The bottom line is, if you want to be whole, if you truly want to be alive, then you've got to do whatever it is you've got to do to find it. And simply finding it, you'll see, is the most important thing. Because once you have, well, there's no turning back. After that, one way or another, your voice will make sure it gets used.

Catch your breath.

The key, once you have it, is to release that energy. Sure you can ignore it, for a while. But ultimately, it will not be suppressed. Your voice will find a way to make itself heard. Like the songbird, your voice will not be caged by your feeble and useless efforts to contain it.

Your efforts are put to far better use by making space for it to thrive. Clear away as much of the chaos and clutter as you can. Breathe in and open up space within yourself where it may dwell.

Here's the thing, and I probably wouldn't say this to just anyone, but we are the light-bearers, the ones who hold the world together. Complacency does not become us. Your voice already knows this. And it is waiting for you to take up the torch.

Let it out.

I'm no different from you. These essays are just one of the ways my voice makes itself known. This page is my teacher and these words are my lovers. Each time I sit down to write, my voice acts as a flower, pushing its way through the clay. Awakening from slumber and breaking through the earth to unleash the beauty of its colors once again.

I know you are afraid. Who isn't? But you need to know that your voice is a butterfly trapped in the cage of your heart. And it simply must be released. There is no other way.

VIII

TIME & *Space*

43

A SPACE BETWEEN THE NOTES

THERE IS A NATURAL ORDER TO LIFE. An in breath and an out breath, expansion and contraction. Everything in nature follows this rhythm. Including us.

The sun rises and sets. We wake and we sleep. The seasons open and close. The Moon fades and swells. The tides ebb and flow. The flowers rest in their swaddled layers and then unfold in their beauty.

The Earth is a sentient being. And she is far more intelligent and powerful than we are. We forget this too often.

There are a few things that attempt to live outside of this natural order. Our global economic system is one of them. Cancer is another.

Cancer grows until it is removed and killed or until it kills its host. Either way, its unnatural growth is short-lived.

You probably see where I'm going with this. Like cancer, global capitalism requires constant growth and feeding. And while it is not in danger of killing its larger host, planet Earth, it is in danger of killing its creator, us.

Music delights us because of the spaces between the notes.

Mother Earth knows more about music than we can imagine. After all, she created it. We only mimic and aspire to her talents.

It could be then, that the shutdown caused by the pandemic is just the Earth asking us to take a breath. Reminding us who is actually running things.

I understand there are real casualties to this crisis. Businesses and lives included. It is also important to remember that there are real casualties to how we've been living, to our addictions to oil and consumer goods of all kinds. Casualties that include the health and wellness of ourselves and the planet. Casualties that could very well include the extinction of the human race. In that light, this could be just the kind of space between the notes we need.

Be well. Take care of yourselves. Reach out to each other often. Take the time for longer conversations, more books, things you want to learn. Take the time to find beauty. And to share it.

44

ROILING IN DOUGH

*On the whole it wasn't the small green
pieces of paper that were unhappy.*
−Douglas Adams

MONEY AND HAPPINESS appear inexorably intertwined in our world. Mostly this is because we tend to mistake the means for the end. Like running a business day after day that only pays for its own overhead, but earns no profit and is not otherwise fulfilling, most of us eventually miss the point.

On the road of life no one wants to run out of gas, but the point of the journey is not just the next gas station. Somewhere between the road sign that says Gas is Everything and the one that says Abandon Your Car & Walk, you'll find the right cruising speed.

Time is a waste of money.
−Oscar Wilde

Money is often used in the same sentence as sex or time or happiness. Though ironically, poor people often have more of all three than the rich. As the saying goes, sex and oxygen are only important if you aren't getting any. But the same is not true of money, often the more money one has the more one thinks about it.

There are those who say that one thing money can buy you is time. But time is only valuable if you remember how to use it. You may have noticed that when most people are not busy on the hamster wheel, they have a tendency to fill the hours with any number of pointless distractions. Television, video games, and fantasy football come to mind.

> *No, not rich. I am a poor man with money,*
> *which is not the same thing.*
> –Gabriel García Márquez

We speak of money in a big, general sense, like we do love sometimes. Even though most of us understand there are many different kinds of love, we tend to think of money in one, big, gray clump. That is to say, we don't really think about it in any meaningful way. Only that generally we want more of it, any kind will do.

Specifically, most of us walk through life not really having any clear idea how much money would be enough for us. Nor is there much thought about the price of money. Most of us would like someone just to write a big fat check that we really don't have to do anything for in return.

Though it really is the last thing most of us without a lot of money want to hear, the rich really do have their own problems. And surprisingly, many of these problems have to do with money. Often money comes with its own handcuffs. And no amount money will buy a set of keys that fit.

> *Anyone who lives within their means*
> *suffers from a lack of imagination.*
> −Oscar Wilde

Add to the list of things money cannot buy: imagination, intelligence, wisdom, character, and love. Perhaps you can get more dates if you have money and a nice car, probably you can get more sex, but love is its own master. Creativity, resourcefulness, curiosity, these things thrive despite money or its temporary absence.

If we think about it, money is no different from any vehicle to take us from A to B. The important thing about money is how you use it. It is a creative force. It is spirit made flesh. It is fuel. It is wind to be harnessed.

I'm amused by the analogy of money to dough. Dough is raw material to be crafted into delightful manifestations of the imagination. Raw dough, by itself, is not that interesting, not that useful. (I'm not talking about cookie dough.) In fact, unless you intend to bake something, there is no reason to worry about having any dough at all.

> *It's easier to feel a little more spiritual*
> *with a couple of bucks in your pocket.*
> −Craig Ferguson

Speaking of spirit made flesh, the irony of the connection between money and spirituality lately is both comical and a little sad. Again, there is an enormous tendency to miss the point.

There is a popular quasi-religious mythology these days based upon the right to collect lots and lots of money because God wants you to have every material thing you've ever desired. Please see the earlier comment about not needing any dough if you don't intend to bake.

I'm not touting the nobility of poverty, suffering, or sorrow. But getting everything you want has never been a recipe for happiness.

> *I have no taste for either poverty or honest labor,*
> *so writing is the only recourse left for me.*
> –Hunter S. Thompson

There are things that money can buy: time, options, better food, good shoes. And being flush is far superior to wondering how the rent is going to get paid.

Still, money is neither good nor bad, it just is. Usually, the problem is a loss of perspective. Or the kind of desperation that keeps the things we want away from us. Also, there are black holes that lie dormant in each of us. And whenever one opens up inside, and we start trying to fill it—whether with food, facebook, or money—the effort is always futile. The more things you try to stuff into a black hole, the emptier it gets. Better to think in terms of flow, of giving and receiving. That is the rhythm of the Universe. The Universe neither hoards nor squanders. It flows.

45

BE FREE

You must learn one thing.
The world was made to be free in.
          —David Whyte

DAVID WHYTE IS ONE OF MY FAVORITE POETS. And this is one of my favorite lines written. It feels good to read. And when I read it, or think it, or say it to myself, it helps me to breathe easier.

But what does it mean, really? What is it to be free? Harder than you might think to answer.

Is it to be physically free to move about the world? Is it to be mentally free to think whatever you want to think? Is it to be free from oppression of some kind? Or is it financial freedom to chase caprice where it leads you?.

For me, one of the things it means is creative freedom. Meaning, freedom to be a full-time creative. Whether that is freedom because my art is self-sustaining or simply that I have the financial independence to be a full-time creative. Whatever the reason, the result is I am able to wake up and make coffee and create all day.

But how do any of us know what we would do with the kind of actual freedom we crave, if it suddenly dropped itself into our life's lap? What if we accidentally squander it?

HAPPINESS IS AN IMAGINARY LINE IN THE SAND

Let me give you an example.

A few months back I was flying back to Reno from San Francisco, where I was working with a team at Stanford Law School on a U.S. Supreme Court case. (It's a long story, maybe I'll write about it later.)

I arrived at the airport early. Ludicrously early, to be honest. This happened because I don't like being late to catch a plane. I finished up with the team at Stanford earlier than planned and so I had a few hours to spare. I could have used that time to wander around the campus or any number of things really. But with the unpredictability of Bay Area traffic and the TSA, I thought it was better to just get to the airport. If I'm early, I reasoned, I'll be able to park somewhere and write. Maybe have a glass of wine.

Turns out, there was no traffic. And I have TSA Pre clearance. The result was I arrived at the terminal crazy early, with hours to spare. So this is the story of what I did with all the freedom I created by my early arrival:

> (1) I made sure I knew where my gate was. As in I didn't just trust the signs, but walked all the way to the terminal offshoot where it was, bypassing more than one perfectly good restaurant along the way, where I could have camped out until time to board my flight;

> (2) Once I had a visual of my gate, I started looking around for *just the perfect place* to hang out for a couple of hours. As if that place exists in an airport. Everything

is crowded and chaotic and there are typically marginal food and beverage choices. Undaunted by these generally known facts, I still wasted a fair amount of time looking at menus and weighing these imperfect options. Also, I did this even though I ate a late lunch on the Stanford campus and was not remotely hungry. Still, I wanted to have the option of a good snack, you know, just in case one glass turns into two;

(3) The wine bar where I want to sit is packed. So I opt for the pub across the corridor. I scan the menu and am pointed to a small two-top table. Which is good, because at a table there is a better chance I'll actually write than if I'm at the bar.

I am approached by a waiter in a short amount of time and order a glass of Syrah. Feeling accomplished for no real reason, I pull out my laptop and open a piece on freedom I've been starting and stopping for a few weeks, fully prepared to make the most of my free time. Soon, though, the waiter appears again and tells me they are out of the Syrah. The right thing to do probably would be to get up and politely leave the pub. But instead, I calmly order a white wine instead;

(4) And now, of course, I'm distracted. I can't help but look longingly across the corridor and think I really should be sitting in the wine bar, drinking the red wine I really want. (In other words, the wine is always redder

in the neighbor's bar.) Not that the wine should have much to do with what I'm doing—or not doing—with my time. The point was to find a good place to write;

(5) Begrudgingly I sit and drink my (white) wine while I get very little actual writing done because I'm not really present at all but imagining some better situation I should be in, and meanwhile my waiter is nowhere to be seen should I actually make the decision to leave;

(6) And I sulk;

(7) And I try over and over to focus on the page and the words that are there or could be there if I just put forth a little more effort;

(8) But really, I can't stop thinking I should be somewhere else. Like maybe that place I passed on the other side of the terminal with calamari on the menu. Yes, calamari and a draft beer would've been a better choice;

(9) But somehow I don't just get up and walk down there. I resolve to enjoy my glass, write where I am planted, and then pay the bill and figure out where else to sit;

(10) Did I mention there's a guy at the next table talking way louder than necessary to the three people sitting right next to him? The one who seems not to understand that he is not in a gymnasium talking to a

large crowd without a microphone (I seem to be at a table next to that guy far too often);

(11) Sitting next to the human megaphone makes focusing on writing way harder than it already was. Also, it turns out I really want that calamari;

(12) The silver lining is that he does provide the catalyst I need to actually relocate so I can finally focus (and have that calamari), and so I quickly finish my wine. And then I have to wait another painfully long time before I can catch my waiter's attention and hand him my credit card, with the universal sign of writing something in midair that means, please bring me my bill;

(13) Can we still use the word *waiter?* ;

(14) Once I pay and I am free to move about the airport cabin once more, I do something interesting. I don't go to the calamari place on the other end of the terminal after all. Instead I check out a deli nearby. I order a chocolate croissant and an Americano to chase it (and the wine). And I sit down to make the most of the rest of my airport freedom;

(15) And then I make another surprising decision. I don't pull out my laptop and work on the piece that is still open on the screen. Instead, I retrieve *The Sun* magazine from my backpack and start reading. And for a few moments, while I am intending to savor the chocolate croissant but mostly am just inhaling

it in spite of myself, I am content. But of course, that doesn't last long;

(16) I slow down and enjoy my coffee more than I did the croissant. But now bad music is following me all over the airport. Like there's a channel called *Every Song You're Sure to Hate from the 80's*. (No Howard Jones, no early U2 or REM, no iconic Madonna, not even Toto.);

(17) Eventually the music drives me out of the deli and into the purgatory of the open airport once more. It is here I realize I need to find a bathroom (I have downed a glass of wine, a cup of coffee, and a liter of water in pretty short order);

(18) After I take a nature break and find a station to refill my water bottle, I go read the board to check on my boarding status again (even though I can easily do this on my phone). And I finally resign myself to just sit in the waiting area and return to the piece I was trying to write;

(19) A few tortured sentences later it occurs to me that this somewhat absurd series of first-world-problem airport events fits nicely into the piece on freedom I am writing. And also makes me ask myself: *Is this what I would do with more freedom? Get stuck in these silly eddies of indecision?*

I hope not. But part of me is afraid of the answer. There's a voice inside that likes to taunt me by implying that if I had the creative freedom I like to talk about, I would squander too much of it in this kind of neurotic paralysis. (The voice likes to bring up these kinds of things that are impossible to counter, because I'm not yet living in this imagined future to know what I would do.)

I remind the voice how much I have actually accomplished in my normal adult life with the very real world time constraints I do have, in spite of all of my flaws. And then I order a whiskey and get back to writing. Not really. But that was funny to say.

I guess my point is this: Authentic freedom is a little intoxicating. And a little bewildering if you are not used to having it.

It doesn't really have much to do with what you would do with a couple extra hours in the airport. In fact, eddying out in two airport hours probably means you don't have enough actual freedom in your life. And that's why, if you find yourself with a small window of it, the pressure to spend it wisely could easily backfire. But the question still lingers out there: What does freedom actually look and feel like?

Here's at least one good answer: Be who you truly are. (It is insane, after all, to think you could be anything else.)

If you have no idea who you truly are (or think you don't), here's another way to think about it: There are thoughts I know you think you have no right to think. You could not be more wrong about that. Those are the exact thoughts that will lead you where you want to be.

There are desires you have that you think are unreasonable, irresponsible, even impossible. They are not. These desires are the thread that will lead you out of the labyrinth of confusion and despair.

And, there are feelings you have that you think are only tiny pieces of life. They are not. With practice you can spend more and more time in the space of those feelings.

As far as I can tell, these things are what freedom looks and feels like. Not how you spend two extra hours in an airport. Not what you may or may not do with a little more spare time.

Because maybe who you truly are actually needs to just fuck off in an airport for two hours in order to recalibrate your creative self and live your truest life. Actually I think that's more like probably, not maybe.

46

A VOID IS NOT SOMETHING YOU FILL

There is an emptiness in me that terrifies me. A deep insatiable hunger. With little warning it can take over, hold me hostage, threaten me, my life, my happiness, my world. I know you know what I mean.

It demands food, wine, coffee, sex: any kind of input, stimulation, entertainment, pleasure. And while I know that none of these will fill me, I will likely try anyway. Again and again. Maybe tomorrow. Maybe today.

I manage this emptiness like one does a gas gage. Keeping one eye on it. Like a bit player in a live play. It comes and goes from center stage. Sometimes the rest of the actors are so good I forget it is there. But it will always be part of the cast.

Sure, we eat because our bodies are hungry. But that is not all. We are also wary of what life may throw at us next. And so we eat for strength, for stamina. We eat because we are weary. And because we want to be comforted.

Warm thick-cut bacon. Fried eggs with runny centers. Melting butter on toast. Dark chocolate and ruby-colored strawberries. Freshly ground coffee with real cream.

Also, clean white sheets. Stuffed pillows. Sumptuous comforter. Soft lips and whisper light tongue to playfully roam your body's wonderland. Time to explore. Space to delight. Presence to enjoy.

Please don't misunderstand. These are all worthy of your time, your taste, your savoring. We incarnated into flesh for a reason. And we neglect these pleasures at our peril.

Essentially, though, we need the ability to function beyond this. Above it and below it. Ay, there's the rub. To honor the flesh and the spirit.

But some of us came in to this life with something different. Something more, I believe. We swallowed lightening in another life. We rode dragons. We parted waters. And we are not so easily contented in this one. Not drawn to the safe, the comfortable, the enough.

Our memories of the heights threaten our livelihood in the valley. We are not believers in all or nothing. Not content to cut off one of our hands. Not complacent enough for sterility.

All the more important for us to locate our boundaries. To trace our own lines in the dirt. If only to give us a place to jump over with some certainty.

It has taken me a very, very long time to realize a void is not something you fill. And that a void is not something to fear. A void is a place of potential, a place to create. A place where we can turn the blank canvas into a playground, instead of a place for stage fright.

Emptiness is a gift. It is not a deficit to be filled. It is a space where we can breathe. It is room to stretch our minds. Our bodies. Our ideas.

Forget what you've been told. We are not what we eat. We are what we create. And all of life is about finding that balance between giving and receiving.

Artists need not be so tortured over their birthright. For me, words are one of the greatest pleasures that exist. Because there is only a probability of them. And so you can eat as many of them as you need. And they won't make you fat. And they won't give you a hangover. And they won't get mad if you read other words.

So it is with paint, canvas, clay, instrument, dance, and song. There is no need to fret because you cannot fill up the void. Indeed, there is no need to try. That is not what the void is there for. It is there to hold space. To echo. To resonate with you, your vibration, the sound of your fire.

The space in a void was created large enough to hold you, your dreams, and your art, and still have plenty of room for your imagination to thrive. I know, like me, your emptiness sometimes threatens to destroy you. But that is not at all what it is there for.

So why not stop for a minute. Take advantage of all that air around you. Take a deep breath. Then stretch out as far as you can. You don't have to fill up any of that space. But it's there for you if you need it.

47

ENOUGH

*Obstacles are like wild animals.
They are cowards but they will bluff you if they can.*
—Orison Swett Marden

THERE IS MUCH TALK THESE DAYS about the ego and its evil ways, about the importance of eliminating or transcending it. It is true we should be more aware of the ego and its tendency towards chaos and distraction. But it is foolish to imagine we can destroy our egos. More than this, it is delusional to believe that eradication of the ego is something we should aspire to accomplish.

Though it has become the all-purpose whipping boy of many a guru, the ego is more akin to the tempting sprite or the trickster coyote of various mythologies. One way in which the ego plays games with us is to continually set up unnecessary hurdles for us to clear. It tells us that if we clear this next hurdle, we'll feel better. If we clear the next one, we will prove ourselves. We will be known as the hurdle-clearer. And all will be right with the world.

But once we're over the hurdle, the ego immediately begins to diminish the accomplishment: It wasn't as high as it looked. Other people have overcome far greater obstacles. Immediately, the ego starts looking for the next thing to "prove" itself. And make no mistake, no matter how high the bar is set, it will not be enough. This is because—among other things—the ego has an attachment fixation with drama.

> *The Master does nothing,*
> *yet he leaves nothing undone.*
> *The ordinary man is always doing things,*
> *yet many more are left to be done.*
> –Lao Tzu

The ego also has a terrible memory and tends to forget its job. The ego's primary job is to be the vehicle for the soul's expression. But for whatever reason, instead of sticking to the task at hand, it has developed a seemingly unending lust for want. And in the perpetual swoon of its desire to desire, it has forgotten its original charge to do the soul's bidding. Intentionally or not, it engages in its own brand of mutiny and re-charters the course of the vehicle for its own means.

No one is certain where this diversion of purpose arose, or even when. Perhaps, like most of us in the modern word, the ego is just easily distracted. But the havoc that follows in the wake of its attention deficit is connected to a great many of the world's problems.

I want to be clear that *want* is not a bad thing. And that desire is an essential component of life. In a way, all creativity is born of desire. And obstacles are also not necessarily bad.

All of us will encounter our fair share. And they tend to build character and identity, to add to our self-confidence, and even help us to evolve as problem-solvers.

> *Whoever is not in his coffin and the dark grave,*
> *let him know he has enough.*
> *–Walt Whitman*

So desire is not bad. Obstacles are not bad. The ego is not bad. The trick is one of perspective. Of balance. Of finding grace. One partner cannot do all the dancing.

In short, life should not be harder than necessary. Next time you are struggling with any issue in your life, ask yourself if the demons you are wrestling are real. Ask yourself if your desires are your own. Is it really something you want? Ask yourself if there are simpler and more substantial pleasures already within your grasp.

The sun rises and sets every day. The Earth is here for walking. The moon puts on a different show every night. The birds fly over our heads and serenade us daily, though we have never paid them anything. The flowers bloom, the leaves change colors, the rain quenches our thirst, the snow paints the landscapes. The wind seeks us out and urges us to dance.

These things effortlessly remind us they are enough. That we have enough. That we are enough.

48

HOW TO NAVIGATE AN INVERSION

Your brain doesn't feel up to the task of thinking. Or even staying awake, really.

A blanket of low-lying clouds drifts over the horizon of your mind and now lay still and peaceful on the landscape there, as if the clouds were napping, with no hint of a breeze to carrying them along their journey. The clouds make you tired. Even though you slept for maybe 7 hours the night before. You still want a nap. Or maybe two days of sleep. You can tell for sure. If you could walk out of the clouds, you would. But wherever you go, the clouds come with you. Like they are on a string attached to your waist.

Sometimes when there is an inversion, you just have to wait it out. Do the best you can until the wind comes along and frees you from the doldrums.

It would be nice if you could just lay down. But you can't. It is only 9:30 am. You have work to do. And words to write. And other adulting stuff waiting for you to grow up enough to see to it. And then later there will be more parenting to do. Even though you are totally not qualified for that. But nobody ever asked to see your resume before you took the job.

And at least every other parent you talk to seems to have the same kind of imposter syndrome. So you just do the best you can. And you try to remember not to yell too much. And not to place your own worries and ambivalence and disappointment about the world on the child. He will have his own things to carry, after all. And maybe the best anyone can do is to show that is it possible to put those things down and just walk away from them. And maybe the child can learn to do it much sooner than you did.

Even now, there are still bags balanced up there on your shoulders, despite all this talk. Because—and you've probably figured this out by now—a lot of the time life is nothing like you thought it would be.

Until those sometimes when it is far better than you ever imagined. It is important to remember that. Even when there are low-lying clouds in your way.

You know if you can possibly slow down, it helps. Just try to take everything as it comes. Even when nothing is coming. To do your best to take that, too.

It helps to remember that you are part of everything and everything is part of you. And so there is really no place to get to. And nothing to get. It is just reaching inside and pulling out whatever is needed. Even if there are low-lying clouds covering almost everything.

HAPPINESS IS AN IMAGINARY LINE IN THE SAND

There is still the quiet gurgle of the stream, the feel of grass under feet, the cool of air as you fill your lungs, over and over and over, thousands of times a day. And the way, even if the clouds are there, if you slow down, you can still put thoughts together, pin words on the page.

Sometimes it seems like maybe it is the words that make the fog to begin with. Or that the fog is made of words. Like you had been neglecting them, and so they started to stack up, causing a word jam that, as it grew, started to look just like a small cloud. And the more you ignore the words, the more the clouds grow, until they cover the valley floor. And all you need to do to clear the path is to start pulling the words down and pasting them to the pages. Over and over and over, thousands of times a day.

IX

INVITATIONS &
Permission Slips

49

FIGHT BACK

Remember your dreams and fight for them.
—Paulo Coelho

MOST OF US WALK around in a quasi-coma state of being. We're numbed up and dumbed down. We've been programmed by society, school, law enforcement, advertising, and social opinion to act a certain way.

Somehow our dreams and aspirations for personal greatness got blended in with the rules of do and don't for the common good. And then the batter was thrown into the oven to make a cake for the masses to eat. The result is a life that looks nothing like you thought it would. Thoreau called it quiet desperation.

Fight back? But I'm a pacifist, you say. Great. A pacifist is one who believes war and violence are unjustifiable. And since that's not at all what I'm talking about, you should be fine. Nothing I'm saying should land you in handcuffs. (Unless they're velvet-lined and you're into that.)

I'm talking about taking down those questions you long ago put on a shelf. About reminding yourself why you are and what you're about. About remembering your childhood curiosities and tracking their scent to your better self. I'm talking about finding your way out.

Now that you know how to dig deeper, you must also discover how to dig your way out. And I'm here to tell you that you can. Yes, it looks like a long way to the top. Yes, you've been down here so long your eyes have adjusted to the (lack of) light. Yes, your muscles have atrophied a bit. Yes, it will be worth the effort.

> *The fight is won or lost far away from witnesses...*
> *long before I dance under those lights.*
> —Muhammad Ali

We are constantly being asked to take up someone else's fight. Our employer's, our country's, and those of our friends and loved ones. In this interconnected world, more and more we're asked to fight the fights of people we don't even know. And I am not here to tell you whether any or all of those are worthwhile. But the most important fight you can choose is the one that ends with you living the life you came here to live.

In big and small ways, along the path of so-called adulthood, we've each let go of so much. We've cut loose parts of our lives that are as essential to us as air and water. The saddest part is that we've traded it all for the cereal prize of an official Grown-Up merit badge. And we're constantly being told what a smart trade that was.

To fight your own fight, the first step is to take a good look around you. Take stock of where you are, what you have, and how you spend your days. As the poet John O'Donohue reminded us, *your life becomes the shape of your days.* Next you have to figure out where you want to be. And if you're one of the lucky ones who already knows, well, then you need to say it out loud. Somewhere that you can hear it. You've got to invoke its presence.

After you've dared to speak its name, guess what, you've actually got to put on the gloves and get in the ring. And fighting your way back to you might take some time. There are no shortcuts. It's taken you a while to hide you from yourself as well as you have. Becoming you again involves creating a day to day habit of being the best you that you can be. And we're definitely not used to that.

I know, that sounds like a lot of pressure. It's okay to admit. With rare exception, society doesn't really want us to be the best we can be. Unless the best we can be looks like a law-abiding, tax-paying, constantly-consuming, take-what-you're-given-and-don't-complain kind of human.

> *Don't fight forces, use them.*
> –R. Buckminster Fuller

Now that I've gone on and on about how much you need to fight the forces, inside and out, that conspire to keep your heart at bay, I'm going to throw a literary wrench into the grinding machinery of your brain. That's right. To really master this thing I'm talking about, this being the you that you dream to be thing, you've got to get in touch with your inner tai chi master.

And to do that, all you really need to do is to get out of your own way. To set down all the have-to, supposed-to, ought-to, need-to mentalities you've been packing around and simply be who you are. Everyday, all the time.

That's not much, I know, just everything. The trick that no one tells you, though, is that it's much easier than it sounds. All you've got to do is sidestep the forces of sabotage and let their own momentum drop them to the ground. Don't worry that you've never practiced tai chi. Once you set down all that other stuff you're supposed to be instead of you, you're going to be a hell of a lot lighter on your feet.

50

GO AHEAD

I'M NOT SURE WHAT YOU'RE WAITING FOR. But let me give you permission. It's been said, you know. This isn't a dress rehearsal. It's happening right now. And now. And now. And it'll keep on happening until, well, it doesn't. (I'm not actually sure that'll ever happen. And if it does, we won't be here to know.)

True story.

As Steve Jobs famously reminded us, we're all dying and we're all going to die. So why not do what you want to with your life. I mean, imagine how silly we're all going to feel years later and wiser when we look back and say, I stayed there for how long?

That's unthinkable.

You know that perfect time you are anticipating. (When you graduate, when the kids are grown, when the bank holds more of your money, when you make that promotion, when you pay off the credit cards, when you lose 10 pounds, when you have more time.) The truth is that time is never going to get any closer than it is. Why. Because it's already here. And here.

And here.

Go on, kiss the girl, write the book, form the band, go out on your own, test drive the car, study the language, save the money, use the passport, take the pictures, paint the canvas, buy the poetry, lace up the running shoes, pump up the tires, paint the walls, plant the flowers, grow the vegetables, try downward dog, sign up for dance class, have a child, say Hi, show up.

Whatever it is that you think you can do, don't just think about it.

Leave.

Your big bank. Your heart-break. Your prejudices. Your anger. Your toxic attitude. Your toxic job. Your toxic relationship. Your stress. Your old ways of doing things. Your self sabotage. Your bad habits. Your clothes you haven't worn for years. Your fear of the unknown.

Be lighter.

Because less is more. And almost everything is inessential. Let me say that again, because it is so entirely counter-everything we are sold in modern life: Almost everything is inessential. Most of all your reluctance to do x, y, or z. Yes, that, most of all. Let it go. Flush it down. Take it out. Recycle it. Compost it. Post it on craigslist. Stack it on the curb. Hang a sign on it. Burn it. Break up with it and change your number.

What is essential is invisible to the eye.
—Antoine de Saint Exupéry

We carry around entirely too much in our days. Like the term baggage, our phones are now great metaphors. The first iPhone was introduced in 2007. Today, most of the planet cannot function without it or some imitation. Being anywhere without our phones, including the restroom, is cause for panic. A casual glance inside any café or coffee house proves that it is our phones that control our lives and not the other way around. Real life does not care about what occupies most of our modern time and attention.

Stay.

With everything that makes you uncomfortable. For all the unnecessary stuff we carry around, there's an equal amount of important stuff we're ignoring. Stop running. Stop avoiding. Stop denying. Stop going the long way around. Stop turning around. Stop making yourself busy. Stop escaping. Just stop.

Be still.

Take Pema Chödrön's advice and lean into it. In fact, take this on as your new daily mantra. No matter what you are feeling. Whether it is reluctance, hesitation, fear, excitement, anticipation, or overwhelm. Stop. Breathe. Sit with it a moment. Lean into it. Become its intimate. Its confidant. Its co-conspirator.

Only then will you know the taste of marrow. Only then can you really understand what it means to seize the day, the moment, this electric now called life. Only then can you truly harvest the sweetness of life. And that, after all, is the point.

To harvest all the beauty you can find. It is your birthright. In this brave new world, we are asked to sow and sow and sow and most of us only manage to take home table scraps in return.

We must forget all that. Because beauty is our birthright.

Ride.

That wave of enthusiasm. Optimism. Gratitude high. Belief in the invisible forces that are really in charge. The ones that playfully shape our lives. Wrap the reins around your gloved hands. Tuck down. Kiss your unicorn on the neck. And give her a meaningful nudge with the heel of your boot. Like you mean it.

Then hang on.

And enjoy. Sure you're scared shitless when she jumps over walls and leaps over crevasses a thousand feet deep. Yes, she's going pretty fast. Yes, it would hurt if you fell. Yes, you'd probably break something. And it would be so totally worth it.

Feel the wind in your face. Watch the trees rush by. Feel the power in her stride. And marvel at the lengths that life will go to just to make you sit up and take notice. Trust your steed. Trust your hands. Trust the reins. Trust life.

51

BE BRAVE

COURAGE IS ONE OF THE FEW MAKE-OR-BREAK THINGS in this world. Nothing great ever happened without courage. And no one ever achieved greatness without being brave. Yes, there is that wonderful, merciful, gift from the universe called grace. But we still have to have courage to believe in grace. And yes, there are those are rare occasions when courage comes from grace.

But we've still got to be willing to use it.

The notion of bravery is very confused. It brings to mind all manner of romantic images. Knights slaying dragons, Hobbits fighting Orcs, pairs of socks battling the dryer. As well as Socrates, Joan of Arc, Galileo, Gandhi, MLK, Mandela, and Aung San Suu Kyi. To name only a few.

These images should be enough to inspire the shrinkingest of all violets, right? Well, not exactly. There's one problem, you're scared. Of course you are. Everyone is. It's okay to be scared. More than this, it is okay to *admit* you are scared. At least to the only person who really matters, yourself. Because one of the greatest acts of courage of all time is to be honest with ourselves.

Are we really skating around on ponds of ego that thin?

That even admitting our fears to ourselves will prove too heavy? That we'll crash through to the ice-cold truth, waking us from our tepid slumber? I say screw that. Slide out to the middle of the ice with a sledge hammer and take a good swing. Easing into the water one toe at a time was never any good. Dive straight in.

It'll be better than you thought in the end.

When we get used to the water. When we no longer are surprised by its revelations. When we can swim around all day, or go in and out at will. When we can become someone who is okay being human. Who not only exudes courage, but passes on the gift of grace.

Then, perhaps, we can tell others. At least one other. One at a time. Until being scared no longer matters. Until it is simply something we do. Like breathing. When it is something we are. Like a boy or a girl. When we understand that this is how it is.

This is how it is to be spirit grappling with flesh.

When we stop running from the things we are. When we care more about finding our path and less about looking foolish. Only then we can begin to really live. Only then we can begin to understand life. And when we understand that being scared is as beautiful as being strong. Then we can begin to see the beauty in all things.

Including ourselves.

All these things we hide from the world. These things that we deny even to ourselves. These are the things that make us human. That make us loveable. That exposed to the light, make us strong, not weak. Real life is messy. No matter who you are. And if we try too hard to hide the mess, we just create new ones.

Life is not like the magazines or the movies. There are heroes and villains, but they live in unexpected places, like our own hearts. When Tolkien said courage lives in unexpected places, he was not just talking about hobbits. And until we let these characters run free, we'll continue sterilizing the joy out of our lives.

To appear foolish is to be free.

And what better thing is there to be in the whole universe than free. Too many of us remain slaves to our egos, our fears, our insecurities. Too many of us will read these words and agree, perhaps even be moved. Perhaps even profoundly. And still we'll go on about our lives doing absolutely nothing about it.

We'll remain hidden.

We'll keep thinking that one day we won't be afraid. One day maybe we'll admit we're afraid. What we don't understand is the freedom we'll know when that day comes.

Most of us live in danger of never knowing that day, though. Most of us believe we are flawed because of our fears, instead of understanding that our fears are what make us whole. And that moving beyond them is easier than we ever imagined.

52

UNRAVEL

Go ahead. Fall the fuck apart.

The idea that we are supposed to keep it all together every minute of every day forever and ever is what's insane. By contrast, falling apart occasionally is normal. But then, modern society is kind of bat-shit crazy if you think about it.

There is an expectation for us to perpetually multi-task our minds out every moment, to work smart for 50, 60, or 70-hours a week, and to raise our children to be whole human beings, all while we keep our relationships healthy, maintain sustainable friendships, stay fit enough to compete with our magazine-cover ideas of ourselves, grow our own food, give back to our communities through volunteer work, and still have enough of a life for *me* time. Does that sound sane?

Of course not. So go ahead, unravel.

What's in a word?

Sometimes, too much.

In the world in which we find ourselves, the word *unravel* sounds an awful lot like unstable, untrustworthy, unsound, undependable. But it doesn't have to. If we can just unthink for a minute. And rewrite a little.

What about the word *unwind*, instead. Go ahead, try it. Unwind. Untangle. Undo. See, it isn't as bad as it sounds. We all find ourselves too bound occasionally by the things, places, people, attachments, and other insanities of modern life. What else is there to do, then but untie the knot? Go on, let go and let yourself untwist. And maybe unshout.

Just because you've gotten yourself all worked up into knots is no reason to stay that way. I'm not saying cut the rope. Although sometimes, if the knots are too tangled, that's not a bad option.

What people will say.

Probably some will say what you think they'll say: *Oh my, look at that. He's come undone. She's lost her mind. They're nuts.* Because that's how it goes. That's how we're programmed. *Can you believe it, he fell off the hamster wheel? What a shame.*

But that doesn't mean you have to listen to those things. Much less believe them. We need to set about collectively unlearning the meaning of some words. Unusing them. And then, rewriting how we talk to each other.

Who knows? I'm willing to bet there are more than a few folks out there who will wish they'd thought of it. They'll wish they had the courage to untie themselves. To spin out of control a little. To fall into a little yard sale of their own.

And then.

Once the untwisting is finished, and things are still, and a bit unorderly, to be sure, what's next? Maybe just let things lay there for a while. It isn't like falling on the ice. You don't have to jump right back up and pretend/hope nobody saw. Stretch out. Relax. Soak up some sunshine.

It isn't a race. And there's no trophy waiting for you at some imaginary finish line for your supreme skill at being inhuman.

What's waiting is likely a massive coronary, a blinding stroke, panic attacks, or a room with extra padding.

Sure, eventually you'll probably need to get back up, dust yourself off, and start again. But hopefully you won't start right back where you left off. Hopefully you'll try a little something different. Like more books, less screens. Less money, more time. More sandals, less suits.

Can't I just stay?

For a while, maybe longer. I'm guessing that eventually you'll probably want to start creating your next design. Lest you forget how to weave altogether. This time, though, try not to use so much material. Try not to make it so tight. Take a few strands, leave a few.

You can always unwind again. You can always change out colors and textures. And it'll be easier to do, the less complicated you make it.

I know this sounds easy. I know it feels hard. I know you think these are pretty words, but it'll never work. Well, maybe it'll work for someone else. But not you. Not now. But why not try? If enough of us say enough, the world starts to change. If enough of us unravel, it starts to be okay. And unraveling becomes a thing that you just do.

Show off.

Now that you've untied and untwisted. Now that you've shaken loose all the threads you didn't need. It's time for show and tell. Go on, strut your new stuff. Walk the walk, turn the turn. Go on, tempt us. Let us all see your new colors.

53

BE THAT

THAT THING YOU WANT TO DO. Do that. That way you want to feel. Feel that. That one you want to be. Be that.

Yes, you. I am most definitely talking to you. The one who thinks these rules don't apply to you. The one who thinks these tricks only work for other people. The one who thinks life is for everyone but you. Or maybe not everyone. But definitely not you. Yes, you. Of course, you.

There will always be reasons why not.

Of course there will. Everything exists. Everything. Including all the things you don't want. But this also means all the things you do want must exist. It has never been any other way.

There will always be the other side of things. There will always be mistakes. And distractions. And bad decisions. And unintended debt. And obligations to this thing and that person. Appointments and all manner of tasks we believe must come first. Of course there will.

But the secret no one tells you is that all of these things bend. They are more flexible than you ever imagined. And you are more magician than you ever thought. And the thing you want more than anything, if you believe in it, then it is the hat, and your dream is the rabbit. And all you have to do is reach down and pull it out.

HAPPINESS IS AN IMAGINARY LINE IN THE SAND

This is all there is.

This is it. And it's real. And the only thing you've ever done that is truly irresponsible is to ignore it. You know I'm right. And you know you've spent your whole life putting obstacles in your way. So believe me when I say your only real job is to get it right. To do that thing. To feel the feeling. To be that. To live the life you can feel but not see or touch. Not yet. But you will.

Forget everything else. Forget all the reasons why not. Forget all your excuses. Forget your broken rhythms. Your missteps. Your hesitations. Your plans that never came to fruition. Forget anger. Forget resentment. Forget everything that came before. Forget your criticisms. Your fear. Your self-doubt. And forgive all these things, too.

Trust me when I tell you that in this new place you are going none of these things matter. I am inviting you to step into a new world. One where none of the old rules apply. It is more than just some Matrix of your imagination. It is every bit as real as the one you've been wallowing in for years. Everything exists. Including this.

Make this the time.

Right now. Give yourself the one present you want more than anything. Do yourself the one favor you've been hoping someone else would do. That life you want. That person you want to be. Be that.

Gather up all your other lists. Scratch off every item but this. Tear up your letter to Santa and write a new one, with only this one thing on it. And then put on the red coat yourself and place it under your tree.

If you do this, your life will change. The world will change. And you will change. Into the one that you want. But you must act. You must believe. And you must be willing to take the chance.

You must have the courage.

Find the courage. Be the courage. Blindfold yourself so you are unable to see the doubts that line your face. And reach down into the dark and grapple until you find the still-smoldering ember of faith. Then grab it with your cold hand. And carry it back to your hearth. To the secret center of your heart. Where no one else has been.

Where you must sit with it. Feed it. Nurture it. Watch it grow. Let its warmth seep into every cell of you. Let its flame reach into the places you guard with you're your very life. Let it ignite all the tiny carefully wrapped bundles of every dream you've ever had. Let it spread. Until its light catches your soul on fire. Then watch it burn.

Forget the drop and roll. Run out into the night of your blindness. A blazing torch of fulfillment. Then set fire to the lifetime of walls you've built between you and it. And watch them burn.

Then dance.

Maybe for the first time in your life. Really dance. Beneath the big blue and black borderless sky. Beyond all fear, all excuses, all doubts. Let your light reach all the way to the stars. And then be still and listen. For the whispered gasp of the stars as they gaze upon your brilliance.

This is all there is. Stop pretending it isn't. Go on. Light it up. That life you want to have. Be that.

54

THRIVE

Come on. You know you want to.

So what's keeping you from it? Is it insecurity, self-loathing, shyness? Let it go. Do you actually still believe that there are people out there who deserve wealth, happiness, and good health more than you? Of course not.

Or wait. Maybe you do. Maybe this is like other universal rules we ignore, like aging. We all have a tendency to think they don't apply to us. We see people around us getting older, getting stuck in ruts, making the same life mistakes. But we are genuinely shocked when we spot those grey hairs on our own heads, and surprised every time we have to turn another page on the calendar. Really, already?

Guess what, the rules of abundance are no different. They apply to all of us. Of course, you know I hesitate to use the word abundance, heavy as it is these days with the weight of pseudo-spiritual babble. But if you bother to look it up, one of the words used to define abundance is "fullness." And that, after all, is what life is. Full.

Pay Attention.

I'm talking to you. Yes, you.

HAPPINESS IS AN IMAGINARY LINE IN THE SAND

I saw you skimming through the beginning of this one, trying to convince yourself I was talking to someone else. Well, I'm not. I'm talking to you. So stop whatever else you're doing, take a break, sit down and pay attention. Get a coffee if you need, or a glass of water, I'll wait.

Here's my point, if you are reading this, then that one-word topic at the top of the page has to do with you. Because that is how the world works. We come to things when it is our time. And if the thing is right in front of you, it's your time.

Speaking of time, I want you to take some of it right now to think about what real thriving could look like in your life. I don't mean the kind of thinking where your mind wanders aimlessly, like when you try to meditate. Or when you're waiting in line at the DMV. Or when you're supposed to be listening to someone, but you aren't, you're thinking about three other things. I mean for you to really set your brain on this question. And then ask why your life doesn't exactly look like that.

Don't ignore the answer.

You know what I'm talking about, the answer that popped into your head as soon as I asked you the question. The one you then dismissed immediately as not being true. Yeah, that one.

You must find the courage to look that answer in the face, just like you would a dream monster, in your most lucid act of dreamworld courage. Because—and get ready, this is the aha moment—that answer is the key to the door you've been seeking for at least half your life.

I know, that sounds dramatic. But it's also true.

Ok, so.

Alright, so we're only 500 words into this piece, and already that's a lot to chew. Stay with me, though. If you want, feel free to grab a quick snack, something to dip in your coffee, maybe. But, come right back. Actually, just carry this with you.

So you've got the answer to both what it would look like to be fully thriving and why you're not. Now, you know what? You've actually got to do something about it.

And I don't mean do something like remember to put it on one of your countless lists of things that silently threaten to plague you for eternity. I mean do something. Anything. One small thing.

And keep doing it. Every day until you are actually finally living on that planet called thrive. And then keep doing it.

Now, tell someone else.

Don't keep it to yourself. Spread the word. Invite more people to the party. Because the more people thrive, the more the world thrives. And the more permission is spread around for others just like you to figure out their own secret to living a ridiculously full and happy life. And who doesn't want that? You know the answer.

X

DREAM MONSTERS & *Awakenings*

55

FEELINGS ARE LIKE CATS

I don't know how I have done it so far. Sewn together the pieces and kept them from falling apart. In the wash, on the line, tumbling down the street, being trampled underfoot.

There's no quantifiable reason for it. I'm not all that suited for doing the things people are willing to pay for these days. I can't write code. Or build a house. Or make erection pills.

I like to help people. But often that doesn't seem to pay that well. Unless you are someone like Tony Robbins. But who has that kind of energy. Still, if I knew anything I could teach someone else, I'd probably put on a workshop too.

Mostly, I like to write. Which seems to be one of the things people are less willing to pay for these days. My dream life looks like waking up in the morning, making coffee and writing. And somehow having all the money I need.

I have a couple of degrees that should mean something. The State of Nevada says it is ok for me to practice law. And so I have done that. And I've helped a few people along the way. But I don't really like the idea of wearing a suit everyday or working someplace where I don't get to choose my clients. And so the paychecks are not always so regular where I work. And I have to create a benefit if I want it.

In theory, the life I've created affords me flexibility, creativity, autonomy, even the ability to make a lot of money. In reality, I get to show up in flip flops some days and take lunch when I want, but I don't take many vacations, and I am often wondering how I'm going to pay for that which must be paid.

Also, I might mention it's possible my brain doesn't always work right. I don't know how common this is. Maybe yours does. Maybe you are able to just do what needs to be done every day, to stay motivated and inspired, meet your deadlines, follow the rules, feed your 401K, exercise, pick up the dry cleaning and the groceries, get the kids when and where they need to be, not drink too much along the way, and get enough sleep.

More often than is comfortable, I find myself half-heartedly reaching for a glass ball in mid-swan dive.

If I could stop what I'm doing long enough to come up with a different game plan than the one I've been running season after season, I might do that. If I could just find the clarity to draft it. And the time to execute it. And the will to see it through.

In all this time, I have managed to do a few things. I mentioned those two degrees. And I passed the state bar. And I've gotten two people off death row. And helped a handful of others turn their lives around.

I've traveled to Europe and Asia. I ran a full marathon. And a bunch of half marathons. I found a girl, got married, and have managed to keep a child alive for more than a decade now. I've also written two novels and received a few literary awards for the second one.

I'm sure there are other things I've done along the way. But there are days where I have no idea how I've done all this, because I feel utterly incapable of being an adult.

And then things like this happen: One morning after I dropped my son off for school, while driving down a crowded street in commuter traffic, I spontaneously cried in my car. Apparently the tears were triggered by something as small as a cover of *Sweet Child O' Mine*.

Sure, I did acid at a Guns n' Roses show once (several lifetimes ago). But I'm pretty sure that wasn't why I cried. It wasn't even nostalgia or longing for those carefree days. Just something about the woman's voice covering the song pierced whatever feeble armor I wear and got me right in the heart before I could catch myself. How on Earth am I to face the rest of this hard scrabble world if a simple song on my morning commute turns me into a river in flood.

Maybe it has something to do with my fear that there is a terrible person who lives inside me. A person who sometimes does things like yell at his son when he gets frustrated with him. Alright, that happens almost daily. He is kind of a nightmare to parent. But he is also an amazing human being, with endless curiosity, creativity, generosity, and independence of spirit and thought. His brightness fills whatever room he is in. (It also has a tendency to blind you if you are trying to corral it in any way.)

Maybe I'm just jealous of him because he's the one who gets to be the child now. The one who does whatever he wants. The one who is not bound by the illusion of time. The one who gets to live in a different realm altogether.

Perhaps what I really want—what we all really want—is to finally wake up from this condition. We want to believe the books we read, the classes we take, the healers we seek out. We want to believe the life hacks we glean from all the podcasts we listen to while driving.

In short, we want to feel alive again.

The trouble is, in order to feel alive again, we are going to have to actually feel. And that really terrifies some of us. Because in this brave new world of bigger, faster, more, we are afraid that those little things called feelings are going to cause us to walk through the day hit by one *Sweet Child O' Mine* after another, and then be utterly unable to function. And that's not an option we want to select.

It also seems like a pretty crappy trade-off, frankly.

Unless you take a step or two back and (like the masters say) become the one who notices the feeling. The same way you would notice a spring flower if you were paying attention. Or a storm cloud, or a snow flurry, or a rainbow.

A feeling is just like a dream monster. The more you're afraid of it, the more it will haunt you. The only thing to do is to turn around and look it in the eye. Shake its hand, invite it to sit down for tea (or whiskey). Then ask it why it has come, what it wants to tell you.

Whether you are trying not to feel anything or trying to feel alive, both are pointless. The feelings will find you. The more you are trying not to feel, trying to ignore those feelings, the bigger they will have to be to get your attention. Also, trying to feel alive is like trying not to think. Both are impossible.

The only thing you can be is open and patient. The only thing you can do is make space. Set an extra place for synchronicity. Without fear. Without expectation.

Feelings are kind of like cats. They'll come when they're ready. They'll rub against your leg for a minute, maybe let you touch them. And pretty soon they'll be ready to go back outside. But if you ignore them, look out. You have to sleep sometime.

56

BE KIND

This may be the single most important thing you can do in your life. Just be kind. Being kind to another creature, human or not, has instant gratification. We instantly feel better about ourselves. Smiling at someone gives us virtually the exact same positive result as if someone smiled at us. All we have to do is think about being kind and it instantly makes us happier.

One of the casualties of the modern age is the lost art of civility. In this age of instant gratification, unfortunately we've forgotten one of the most gratifying acts of all, common courtesy. There is not a single person who can say this rule doesn't apply to them. Though everyone from professors to politicians forget it. Whether you are serving food or sitting on a modern throne, you need to be more kind more often.

Whatever your occupation, be it a magistrate or a metal worker, a senator or a city councilperson, a janitor or a judge, your first job is to be kind. Whether you're in the grocery store or online, in traffic or on the phone, be kind. Be kind to everyone you meet, no matter the circumstances. Be kind to your co-workers. Be kind to those who work for you. And be kind to those you work for. Most of us work for someone. And far too many of us forget this far too often.

HAPPINESS IS AN IMAGINARY LINE IN THE SAND

Police officers be kind to those you stop. And drivers be kind if you're pulled over. Politicians be kind to your constituents, even though it's not election time. Neither the black robe nor the council chair change who you are. But if you're not careful, they change who you think you are. Be mindful that words have power. And be kind to all who come before you, be they counsel or convict, whether they're being sentenced or seeking justice.

Smile while you're mopping the floor. Smile when you're behind closed doors. Even though you don't have to. Especially because you don't have to. Make up your mind to be someone who smiles at people on the street. Even if they don't smile back. Remember you have a choice. You always have a choice. You can always choose kindness.

It might help if I explain that I'm not naïve. I'm not here to blow unicorns up your skirt. In addition to being a writer, I'm a world traveler and a criminal defense lawyer. That last one means I often see people at their lowest. I know that life is hard. I read the news. The world can be ugly and scared and mean. I know about political and economic and judicial systems that too often crush the human spirit. And I understand that even the people in charge of those systems are broken.

I think that part of the reason we're not more kind, more of the time, is because we're fed up. We're tired of the selfish, tight-assed meanness that we see in the world, in government, in our own neighborhoods. But being fed up and lashing out because you're fed up doesn't help. It only adds to the lack of kindness.

Yes, the world is kind of fucked up. But it's also beautiful. There's an old tale of two wolves that battle inside each of us. And the young child who wants to know which wolf wins. The answer his grandfather gives him is important to remember: The one you feed.

Let's all sign up for local farm baskets for our kindness wolves. Baskets filled with wonderful things grown and raised by wonderful people with wonderful intentions on clean land. Let's buy extra baskets for our friends and neighbors, so they can feed their kindness wolves good stuff too.

Some of you may still dismiss this as utopian dreaming. But it's really not that crazy. Just stop being afraid of what people will think. Kindness does not make you weak. Or stupid. Or naïve. That's where meanness comes from. Meanness is a defensive tool. It's a weapon for those not brave enough to put down their shields.

What I am saying is not new. And I am far from the first to say it. Plato, Lao Tzu, Gandhi, Einstein, Anne Frank, Emerson, FDR, Kahlil Gibran, Dalai Lama, Mark Twain, Aldous Huxley, Kerouac, Vonnegut, and countless others have offered us this same wisdom. It's up to us to accept it. It's up to us to remind each other. It's up to us to practice it. It's up to us to pass it on.

The remarkably simple but profoundly transformative truth is that each and every moment we are free to choose how we show up. And remember that the world is a mirror. Kind people create a kind world.

57

LIGHTEN UP

A person without a sense of humor is like a wagon without springs...jolted by every pebble on the road.
—Henry Ward Beecher

Happiness is not something that falls from the sky. Paraphrasing the character Hobson from the movie *Arthur*: Happiness is a tie you cannot steal. Happiness is a tie you are going to have to work for.

Like you, I have days where it is hard to find my way to happiness, or to contentment, or even to the blank page. Even though there are other times when I am so swiftly in the flow I think I will surely ascend this plane.

But true and lasting happiness is not subject to the vicissitudes of weather, hormones, or circumstance. It is a matter of training the mind *and* the heart. It is a matter of teaching ourselves to laugh, of practicing light-heartedness, of remembering to keep checking our perspectives and to travel a little lighter.

All day, every day, Life hands us countless opportunities to laugh. But mostly we see them as small failures and frustrations. From the unwelcome alarm clock to the sinkful of dishes, the crowded calendar to the congested commute, we wish away so much of our days. Instead of embracing the poetry, absorbing the small details, and learning to laugh at ourselves more often.

> *I think the next best thing to solving a problem*
> *is finding some humor in it.*
> –Frank A. Clark

I have a son who is a master teacher. Minute by minute he challenges me to walk my talk. Often Ghandi-esque in his resolute defiance (though not always as peaceful), he forces a constant need for a new perspective. Whether it is his endless distractions when time is already short or his refusal to be controlled, no matter the method, he is bent on breaking my will and on helping me to recognize the downright absurdity of my carefully constructed self-image.

Love is as close a word as has been discovered to describe the magnificent magic of children. Free of social constructs and unburdened by the overstuffed baggage of adulthood, children are able to simply *Be* far better than most yogis I've met. They challenge our well-structured lives and even our best intentions for their well-being. They effortlessly deconstruct our worldviews and constantly pull off our adult masks.

Somehow children innately know that the very things you believe protect you are also your greatest barriers to freedom. But you don't have to be a child to adopt a more playful mindset.

One thing I've noticed is almost all adults are really just children with mortgages. They throw the same tantrums and suffer the same slings and arrows of the fragile ego. So maybe we are not so far from our inner child as we may think. Why not take advantage of this to adopt a more childlike view of the daily world?

There is a lot of talk these days about enlightenment. But there may be a great deal of misunderstanding about what that word means. I'm pretty sure it doesn't mean fairies are going to fly out of your butt and grant your every wish. It is likely closer to an understanding that we are each infinitely more powerful beings than we realize. Which also means we are capable of throwing all manner of obstacles in our way by taking ourselves and our lives too seriously.

Sometimes you will be happy and sometimes you will be sad. Experiencing emotions is part of being human. But Life is also absurd. And it is damn near impossible to deal with that fact unless you have trained yourself to laugh about it. More often.

When we are able to laugh at ourselves and the absurdity of life's theatre more often, we are also able to have more compassion, for our fellow humans and ourselves. In other words: *Absurdity is the soul of compassion.*

58

WHAT ARE YOU LAUGHING AT?

The earth laughs in flowers.
—Ralph Waldo Emerson

I SAT DOWN TO WRITE SOMETHING about the Harvest season, about the rhythms of the Earth. About the importance of gathering what we have sown. About Fall colors, wool sweaters, and wood smoke. And then I did something really stupid (not that uncommon, truthfully) and I ended up laughing out loud at myself.

In this space between the words, I saw a glimpse of a person about to take himself too seriously. I decided to accept the gift that laughter handed me, to throw away the map, get off the bus and just wander. And that made me smile.

If we couldn't laugh we would all go insane.
—Robert Frost

Though I've collected my share of responsibilities in recent years, I'm a guy who relishes the chance to do the unexpected. I thrive on a carefully cultivated path of responsibly pursuing what I'm sure looks to others like the irresponsible.

Which is precisely why a piece on laughter is so perfect. Laughter seems like exactly the kind of behavior that grown ups and other pseudo-responsible types neither engage in nor abide. It is the kind of thing we were always in trouble for in school. Which may be why we still always feel like we're getting away with something when we are laughing.

As it turns out though, laughter is one of the most healthy and responsible things we can do. Medical researchers and yogis alike embrace laugher as a miracle cure for all sorts of ailments and as the secret to happiness.

> *Laughter is the shortest distance between two people.*
> —Victor Borge

In a world where the biggest challenge has always been the building of bridges between people, it seems that Victor is right. Laughter is a universal language. And it is a universal icebreaker, instantly allowing us to drop our defenses.

Laughter eludes definition and ignores decorum. Laughter slips through the slats in our fences and unlatches the gates of inhibition. Laughter undermines our efforts to take ourselves seriously. And really, who doesn't need more of that.

> *Whoever undertakes to set himself up*
> *as a judge of Truth and Knowledge*
> *is shipwrecked by the laughter of the gods.*
> —Albert Einstein

All our ignoble institutions, the same ones that are crumbling under their own obscene weight—health care, the law, politics, banking—could stand to treat themselves to a good laugh or twenty.

All the pious and the pretty, the judgmental and the damned, the iconic and the unknown, ought to make laughter their new mantra. We could all make revolutionary leaps in evolution with this one simple act, this surrender, this letting go.

> *Laughter is poison to fear.*
> –George R. R. Martin

I have written about our absurd fear of the unknown. Laughter drags those fears out into the street, out into the daylight where they can no longer have any hold on us. Laughter saves us from ourselves. And gives us back to each other.

The thing we can't do in class. The thing we try to hide with our hands, by turning ourselves backwards, by leaving the room. The thing we feel almost guilty for doing. Yes, that thing has the power to save us.

59

THE SHIFTING WORLD

The Earth is not the only thing that experiences quakes.

Our world shifts, inside and out. Constantly. Sometimes it is dramatic, sometimes it's agonizingly slow. But the seismic waves never stop rolling. Sometimes the ocean is peaceful, sometimes it throws a tantrum, but it never stops moving.

When we think of change we usually think of BIG change. And for most of us the word itself brings up some measure of fear. But if we think about it, slow change can feel a lot like an eddy. Better for the universe just to rip off the bandage and toss us into the next set of rapids. Either way, there's no point in resistance.

> *We must die to one life before we can enter another.*
> —Anatole France

A few years ago we had an unusual amount of earthquakes where I live. And so I started paying attention to a website that keeps track of these things. What I discovered is that there are actually quakes happening all the time. Instead of the planet being completely static and then suddenly experiencing dynamic events, there are constant little readjustments.

The cause of bigger earthquakes is often what is called a fault movement. An interesting choice of words. But fitting when we consider it has to do with inflexibility, with guarding a weak spot, building too much scar tissue around a wound. And when the world pushes on that spot, long enough or hard enough, snap.

Being essentially made of the same stuff as the earth, humans are really no different. So when we hunker down and focus too much on staying safe in our caves for too long, it often takes a tragedy to move us off our square. To break this pattern, we must become accustomed to feeling a little off center, ungrounded, in flux. We must, more than ever on this hyper-changing planet, learn to develop our sea-legs.

Interestingly, the more shallow the earthquake, the more damage it does to infrastructure. This metaphor presents us with an idea that is counter-intuitive to say the least. But it is at least worth considering. What if most of the things that really rock our worlds are not so important after all? Or to look at it another way, what if our inflexibility with life's shifts and turns actually causes us the biggest heartaches.

Anyone in a longish-term relationship knows what I'm talking about. Crumbs on the counter, lid off the toothpaste, toilet paper roll on backwards, towel on the floor, taste in art. Wait, never mind about that last one, that's probably a deal-breaker. The point is that the rigid mental concepts we've assigned to all these areas of our lives, the things we think are helping us understand and navigate life, these are the very things that will cause our foundations to crack and our buildings to fall.

> *When people are ready, they change.*
> —Andy Warhol

Whether there is a parallel in shallow flexibility or not, one thing all larger quakes have in common is the aftershock. An aftershock is a ripple effect that, like a visiting drunken relative, lingers too long and tends to repeat itself too much. The more the inflexibility that leads up to the shift, the more aftershocks there will be. And the more those around us will feel the fallout.

Maybe an earthquake is the planet's way of trying to remind us that resistance to change is not only futile, but ultimately more damaging than change itself. When even mother earth needs to hang on to her past self in some ways, we can hardly blame ourselves for our inability to stay present. Still, I think she's trying to tell us that the more we let go, the better we'll be.

The truth is we cannot hold on to any of it, not even for a minute. Not because we are not strong, but because nothing can ever be kept from where it is going. I'm sure that's by design, so we won't miss the next daring adventure, silent moment, or glimpse of beauty.

60

DON'T STOP

Don't do it. I know you want to. But don't.

I know you are tired. I know the world seems too crammed full of other people's stuff for there to be any room for you and your dreams. But I beg you to keep looking. The space where you'll thrive is out there. It might be right where you are standing. Or lying huddled in a ball. Or wishing you were.

I know it is out there because you exist. If there were no room for you, you wouldn't. So since you do, there must be. Just keep going.

I wish I could offer you something more. I wish I could take you by the hand and lead you to that place, the one the universe is patiently waiting for you to find. But I'm busy trying to sweep, to rearrange furniture, to paint my own walls. I'm digging under the cushions for change and trying to remember which book I hid the money in so I can pay the rent. I'm second-guessing whether this is actually my space after all.

But even if it isn't, it doesn't matter. I can't stop now. And neither can you.

I know about the voice in your head that keeps telling you to grow up. I know because I hear it too. It graffitis the walls around town and writes its manifestos in magazines and on billboards. It wants you to stop. Because if you don't stop, little by little there will be less room for the meaningless bullshit that feeds it.

Your soul is important. Not just important like an appointment with the eye doctor is important. Important like the birth of the universe is important. Like the speed of light. It doesn't have to squeeze itself into the tiny margin your grown-up world has designated for it. Your voice matters. It doesn't have to keep quiet, to speak only when spoken to. You have the same right to take up space here as anyone.

Stand your ground. Don't allow yourself to be bullied. Look the dream monsters in the face and demand their respect.

I know. I know you just want to sit down, lie down, stay down. I know you want to cut the rope and just let it all go, the dreams, the hope, the endless hanging on. But don't.

I know how tempting it is to believe your thoughts, when in your exhaustion they tell you you've been kidding yourself all this time. I know you think the world has passed you by. You think you are too late to the game, that you should have started at 25, 17, 12 years old.

I know you think you are too old for this shit.

But I need you to hang on just a little longer.

I know this isn't what you really want to hear. You think, if you could just take a little nap, everything would look a little better. But I know if you go back to sleep, you might not wake up again.

And if you don't wake up, there'll be no way for you to tell us about your dreams. You won't be able to smuggle the words back from the other side. And that's a big deal. Bigger than you think. Because we need those pages in order to tell the whole story. Without your words, the story goes untold, consciousness stops expanding, the universe stops unfolding. And that can't happen.

So please, don't stop. We need your dreams. You are not being selfish in wanting the things that feed you, in needing them. And you're not making it up.

So stand your ground, put down roots, stretch out, shop for furniture, lamps, a comfortable chair. Breathe deep and long. Take in as much air as you need. You're not being greedy. You are doing the universe's bidding.

It's not just okay to live the life you've imagined, it's what is required. You don't have to ask permission. You already have authority, autonomy, legal rights. Stop hiding. Get up and turn on the lights. Open the window, pull back the curtains, let us see your face, your hair, your nakedness.

It's okay to be happy. It's more than okay.

It's why you're here.

XI

TRANSFORMATIONS & *Accidental Discoveries*

61

SPLINTERED ONENESS

I WAS GOING TO WRITE something about Saint Patrick. Something about the metaphor of the clover. How he used its three leaves as a bridge to cross the chasm of organized religion's dogma and reach the pagans on the other side. To talk to them about the divine in nature, in even something as small as a clover. The three leaves, the Trinity. One thing containing many.

But my voice decided to take a holiday without scheduling it with me first. It knows what I believe about the power of words. About their absolute essential nature. About their heft and their lightness. About their gravitational pull on some of us. And also about how they are not real. They are metaphors. I think it was this last part that sealed my fate.

It is true. The world is never only one thing. Everything is like St. Pat's clover. Filled with metaphor and potential. Having different meanings to each of us. This is why words are so important. And not just to me. In a world as fractured as our own, the ability to reach across the distance between people is as important as air.

I was also going to write about the snakes. You know, the legend is that there are no snakes in Ireland because Saint Patty drove them out. It's a nice story. But it's probably not true. Geologic studies show that there have never been snakes in Ireland.

Which is a shame, because snakes provide the perfect metaphor for change. And I wanted to write about change. About our universal need for transformation. About how becoming stuck, getting depressed, and even the sudden disappearance of a voice, could be signals that we need to shed some skin of our own.

But then my morning was filled with the usual chaos of spilled juice and spiked tempers, stubbornness and spinning minute hands. Eventually escalating into a weeping and still-pajama-clad boy curled up on the floor beside the clothes I've been trying to coax him into for half an hour. It is only a matter of time until they kick me out of the parent club.

On the way to school—hopelessly late, but clothed, lunched and backpacked at least—I think of all the ways our lives can go off track, one little or big thing at a time. Maybe it's an illness, a layoff, or a breakup. Or maybe it's just a pile-up of little things like impossible schedules, late fees, bad school reports, and the political erosion of progress. Sometimes all before breakfast.

Eventually I safely deliver my child to his classroom and waive apologetically at his teacher. Back in my car, I am not feeling my best self. And it is not my voice returning from vacation, hat in hand, that knocks at the door of my mind, but all these daily little failures and frustrations. In this state, I do not see the beautiful snow on the mountains or the sun painting the morning clouds. Instead, I look around and see all the sad sights there are to see in any city.

A wave of fatalistic fantasy crashes into me, and I see myself slam into the nearest concrete structure. Splintering into tiny unrecognizable shards in a flash of light and metal and bone that simply evaporate into the desert morning air. Into oneness. And then nothing. Just silence. Sweet empty silence. But a friend's voice in my head interrupted gently asking me a question he'd offered before, *What, in this moment, is lacking?* And I realize I couldn't possibly know what was going on in this moment, because I wasn't there. And so I breathe in. And then out.

And then I know that this image, too, is a metaphor. Like the magical clover. Because all things exist in one, the oneness cannot be destroyed, no matter how it is splintered. And I think again about Patty's snakes. Leaving their old skin behind. Remaking themselves. And about the undeniable power of transformation. And I know now where I am. And what I must do. We cannot remain the same if we really want to live. Our old skin cannot hold us.

62

LIFE WOULD LIKE YOUR FULL ATTENTION

OPEN YOUR EYES, as well as your heart and mind. The Buddhists say that awareness is the most important thing. Actually, as the teaching goes, it is the three most important things: attention, attention, attention. Hiding in plain sight in that word is (the sound of) the word *tension*.

Now, I suppose that when one has become a master, the tension part of attention goes away, and there is only relaxed awareness. But I'm not really qualified to talk about that. Knowing my limitations, I'm going to recruit a little help on this subject from David Foster Wallace.

Wallace once told a graduating class the story of an old fish swimming by two young fish, greeting them and asking, "How's the water?" After a while, one of the young fish turned to the other and said, "What the hell is water?" His point being that the most important things in life are often the most obvious and also the hardest for us to see.

I agree that we lean too heavily on our own ideas, beliefs, expectations, worldview, in order to get through the day. The irony is, these are also the very things that keep us from living the lives we want, that keep us from true happiness. And yes, that seems like a really cruel joke for life to play. But it doesn't make it any less true.

Life is dangerous.

There are things that happen in life that cause us to pause. Including death or sudden violence. And so many things that don't. Like the patient presence of beauty all around us. Or, using the fish analogy, the air we breathe all day and night. Every day and night. Our whole lives.

I can't explain exactly why, but in recent years the unexpected deaths of people like Phillip Seymour Hoffman, Robin Williams, and Anthony Bourdain shook me. They were each just something I didn't see coming. Something senseless. Something that happens in a dream. And then you wake up and think, that was weird.

I was a little too embarrassed to write about it. I mean, lots of innocent people die every day all over the world in terrible circumstances. Why make something out of the death of these celebrities? But whether it is the death of someone personally in your life or someone who is a fixture in modern culture, it is unsettling.

More recently, one of my best friends, someone I saw and talked to almost daily, died in a bicycle accident. For 25 years my life was entwined with his. I originally met him in the little unconventional restaurant he owned, my favorite in town. For the last 10 years my office has been in the small building he owns in Midtown, a delightful place with an atrium and a tiny pond in the middle. He inspired me to ride a bike, built a town bike for me, made the desk where I am typing these words. Our kids went to school together. He built things for my house. He made the steel railings for my partner to hold onto while she walked up and down the stairs when she was pregnant with our son. He was one of my heroes. Our friendship transformed me.

Life is uncertain.

Just like the fishes' water or the air we breathe, there is much we take for granted. Like our ideas of the world, we somehow think that we have to take these things for granted, you know, in order to function. In order to do the so many other things there are to do in a day.

The masters would say this is folly thinking, that this constant ignoring we do is part of the grand illusion. It is the opposite of awareness. That the real reason we find life so difficult so much of the time, is that we have stuffed away most all of the things that are essential to life, in favor of the illusion.

I believe death rocks us because it temporarily wakes us from our slumber. Whether it is the death of a personal loved one or the death of a bright light we only know from a distance, we relied on them somehow, like water or oxygen, to provide us with the illusion of permanency.

Life is beautiful.

The morning after I found out about my friend, I slowed down a little. Instead of being hurried about getting my son where he needed to go and thinking about the day's work, I just slowed down and was really here. As I watched my son get ready. As I asked him for the fifth time to brush his teeth. As we gathered our things. As we walked to the car. As I checked if he fastened his seatbelt.

I slowed down enough to watch what was happening. I saw him. I saw us. I was there for it. I savored every little thing. As if each moment were a delicious tiny meal.

I hadn't slept that well the night before. We were late getting our morning going. And all the usual morning logistics had to be navigated. But somehow these things didn't get to me. A smile rose up on my face even as I was struggling to get dressed and to collect all manner of things for our day. I smiled because I had remembered to be here.

We must let life happen. We must allow it to get our attention. To wake us up. And then we must do our best to stay awake. That is the whole point. Stay awake. Shake others awake. Grab them and hug them and kiss them. Show them the stars and the equally incomprehensible numbers of leaves of grass right in their own backyard.

Get down in the grass and see how we would look if we were tiny bugs. Stare into each other's eyes and wonder at the remarkable ability we have just to see things, how many billions of organs and tissues and membranes and cells and firing neurons it takes just to look at the world, just to gaze upon a bee getting drunk on a sunflower.

Life Doesn't Want You to Get Used to Any of It.

We get used to the light. Here in the high desert, we get used to more than 300 days of sunshine a year. So when it rains, we pay attention. I love the rain, more than I can express. And I imagine if I lived somewhere like Seattle or Portland or London, I'd get used to the rain in the same way.

There are people and things who shine brighter than others. And we need their light. Their light is important to remind us of beauty, of humor, of lightheartedness, of grace. But when we are able to slow down, to really be here, we realize what Rembrandt knew centuries before, that all things are made of light. As Master Ajahn Chah taught us, the glass is already broken, so enjoy it all the more. This is the balance of the spiritual and the material worlds, a practice that is essential for us to master if we want to suck all the marrow from life.

Life is random. Life is complicated. Life is often unforgiving. And we must each live it anyway. And I don't mean live it as if it were a chore, something to be endured, survived. I mean dig in, get muddy, howl at the moon, take pictures of sunsets, play in the rain, make love, savor your food, smile as much as you can. And cry when you're sad.

Live it despite the fact it sometimes pisses you off. Live it and pay as much attention as you can muster. So when a light goes out, as even the sun will do eventually, instead of mourning, you can say thank you, because you were really with it when it was here. And you didn't miss anything.

63

THE ART OF HOLDING HANDS

SOMETIMES MY SON SPONTANEOUSLY holds my hand. We might be getting out of the car and starting to walk towards a café or a store or summer day camp. And he will just slip his hand into mine, of his own volition. And then really hold it like he means it. Until we cross a threshold into the place where he and his attention are captured by something else, and he is off.

Or maybe he'll give me a hug. Or make a small piece of art just for me. Or leave me a scribbled note in my bag. Or write in the dust on my car window. (Yes, my car windows are often that dirty. But I have at least three jobs if you count parenting, so maybe cut me a little slack.)

What I mean to say here is there is nothing like that feeling. Like your hand being held by a smaller hand. A hand that happens to belong to someone you helped bring into the world. Someone you are charged with guiding through its storms and sun. These are the things. The things that are unlike any other things.

Let me add this. My son has never been an easy kid. In addition to a bright mind and a generous heart, he has an oversized will, forged of absolutely unbreakable stuff. Japanese steel, I'm pretty sure. And though he is kind of a little guy, nothing else about him is small. His curiosity, his exuberance, his energy, his personality, his voice. He questions everything. And he has a surplus of attention. Pretty much all the time.

Also, even as a baby, he did not want to be swaddled, or held too long. He was restless for adventure from the moment he took on this breath we share. All of which, I hope with everything inside me, will make him an amazing adult. His indomitable will. His keen eye for justice. His inability to take anyone's word for almost anything, without his specialized peer review. Most days he is a jaguar trapped in a living room, as Greg Brown would say.

All of which is to also say that raising him, trying to shepherd him through the world, has been a bumpy road. When the simple act of brushing teeth before bed can take 45 minutes, even Mary Poppins might unravel a little. There are days, of course, when I want to give up. When I am convinced beyond doubt that he has chosen the wrong father. That the fabric I am made of is not the kind that is strong enough to hold him. That my box was damaged in transport (you know the kind that arrive with after-market tape holding them together) and I am now missing critical parts of the intricate machinery of fatherhood that were supposed to be included.

But then he rights himself somehow. And I get up from the puddle on the floor. And the teeth get brushed. And the book gets read. And the lights go down. And he tells me goodnight. And that he loves me. (Despite my missing pieces and torn fabric.) And the world keeps spinning.

And, more poignantly, he is growing up. The hand-holding, the crawling up into my lap, the wanting me to carry him, these are the brief glimpses I still get into the land of milk and honey. Into a kind of temporary parenthood Nirvana. Because we will eventually cross an invisible line beyond which he will no longer reach for my hand.

Beyond the sadness of that loss lies the question of how I will ground him without these physical connections. Because most days I suspect that what he really needs is a dad who is a Jedi Master with an MFA in creative parenting. One part Jedi. One part artist. I suspect he may actually be a Jedi Master who has come to train me. While the Jedi part may be out of realistic reach, the artist part I can do. In any case, my being more of an artist and less of a lawyer serves us both.

To make art requires us to be vulnerable enough to tear out our hearts and hold them up for the world to see. And then to be strong enough to remain standing if the world doesn't fall in love with us

As it turns out, it is pretty much the same with parenting. So these two paths I have chosen, artist and parent, are either going to kill me or forge me into one mind-blowingly enlightened being.

I've discussed the path of the artist. The path of parenting (especially spirited children) is similar in many ways. We are charged with the same kind of work. We must have the confidence to follow our own voices and to be focused enough not to lose them in the strong pull of the crowd.

Mainstream culture creates a mighty current. One that will tow us effortlessly along with it if we are not mindful of our course. It is important to listen to our voices and to find our own way. If for no other reason than when we are caught up in the crowd, there is no space for some little person to get close enough to us to reach up and take hold of our hand. And it is worth any amount of current resisting so we can feel that.

64

THE EARTH IS AN ENLIGHTENED MASTER

The Earth is a sentient being. Not only is this not hyperbole, it is an understatement. The Earth is not only sentient, she is far more intelligent, conscious, and powerful than we are. We forget this to our peril. And in our boundless ignorance, we often simply deny it.

Here's a few reminders of her power over us. A $300,000 sports car becomes a paperweight in an ice storm. A 3 million dollar home turns to toothpicks in a tornado. A 30 billion dollar aircraft carrier becomes scrap metal at the hands of a tsunami. The rainforest can swallow a six lane highway project, along with trucks two stories tall, in a matter of months. And leave no trace that any of it existed. (For real, just ask Brazil.) Indeed, the current climate crisis threatens to erase our species from Earth's history forever.

The more remarkable thing about the Earth, though, is her attention to the smallest details: The petals of an orchid, the antennae of an ant, the spiky fins of a lionfish. And her mastery of alchemy: Turning sunlight into food, minerals into colors, death into life.

Humans lose their perspective all the time, foolishly believing the universe not only revolves around them, but is organized for them. The known universe was born somewhere around 13.8 billion years ago. Or maybe it just woke up from its slumber then. Nobody really knows, none of us having lived that long. For all we know, the known universe is but a thin strand of hair on a magnificent beast. One that lives in an even greater world of its own.

Somewhere around 4.54 billion years ago, planet Earth was born. Plus or minus 50 million years. (How's that for perspective, the Earth is old enough that 50 million years on either side of its possible origin is relatively unimportant.) And then about 300,000 years ago homo sapiens arrived (again, give or take), thanks to a few millions of years of evolution from our more primitive ancestors. A nanosecond, really, on the universal timeline.

The point is this. Life predates us by a considerable amount of time. We are neither the beginning nor the end of life's journey. It is possible we are but a blink of life's eyelash. It is also possible we are simply garden critters that showed up one summer on Earth and then never returned after the winter.

Our human advances in science and technology have rendered only the faintest of understandings of Earth.

What the moss and mushrooms know alone would take us generations to distill. And how they, the pine needles, and the butterflies are interconnected, along with everything else, may never be fully within our grasp. It is time we act accordingly. It way is past time.

And not just with regards to our home planet, but the other neighbor critters who live here. Be they human or winged or four-legged, or, you know, snakes. The arrogance (and the delusion) that any of us have any kind of superiority—over the Earth or each other—is based purely in a certain lazy ignorance. Our prejudices and hatreds of one another are just smaller microcosms of this larger universal ignorance.

Also, wherever it began, life has a propensity to create. Always has, as far as we can tell. In this way, modern humans are a bit of an anomaly in our tendency to destroy more than we create. We are part of life, after all, and so it is our nature to create.

One way we can figure out how to stay part of Mother Earth's ancient and vastly intelligent ecosystem for a bit longer is to do more creating. Not necessarily creating more humans, as it appears we are not experiencing a shortage. Instead, let's create more sustainable ways of life, more sanctuaries for those at risk, more bridges to one another, more awareness of our unique, but marginal place in the world.

The more we know, the more we realize how little we know. It is time we wake up from this dream of our own advanced intelligence. It is time we start listening to the Earth and to each other. It is way is past time.

65

FEATHER IN THE WIND

Some days we are the wind. Some days, the feather. Nothing is guaranteed from one day to the next.

To be the wind requires a strong will, a sense of purpose, a willingness to affect change. To be the feather requires a lightness of heart, an act of faith, the willingness to let go.

Life does not come with instructions. No matter what they teach you in church. No one can tell you what is right for you, where your path will lead, how to find your way home.

There are times in each of our lives when we simply get lost. Because that is life. And I don't know about you, but when I am the most lost, there has never been anyone on the horizon with a flag waving me to shelter.

The older we get, the more we realize how little we know. Our knowing turns from youthful certainty towards things like the realization that nothing is forever. That everything is on its way to someplace else, something else.

The strength of a feather in the wind is its ability to let go. To float. Viewed differently, its strength is its inability to stay fixed, stationary. This condition ensures it a life of beauty, grace, adventure.

We should all be so lucky.

Like many other times in our crooked-path of becoming, these are challenging times. But I want to urge you to take up the challenge. You are more up to it than you think.

Be the feather in the wind. Tossed about by the daily news, the disheartening knowledge of how much fear and hatred is out there, the vicissitudes of history. And bring others joy by the beauty of your lighthearted dance.

Because beauty will save us. In the end, light-heartedness, joy in the simple act of living, and the brave act of loving, these things will give us back to ourselves. They will remind us who we are. And what we can do together.

There are no certainties except uncertainty. Tomorrow I may not be here to write any more essays. It is likely far worse and far better things will happen. Still other things will not happen at all. Or at least they won't happen as we think.

And even the bad things may not be the tragedies we imagine. Because all this uncertainty is the compost that creates the fertile soil of imagination, of creation, of beauty.

Life is built on top of death. Light depends upon dark. And up upon down. Wholeness is just that. It is not the half moon.

In order for us to truly evolve, to move beyond this phase of us versus them, to create the brotherhood of man that Lennon imagined for us, we must let go of our ideas of what we thought life should look like. We must imagine all of the things it could look like.

We must be brave enough to allow life to change us. And to keep kindness in our hearts as we float upon the winds of change.

Every time I sit down to write I am trying to change my life. And the lives of others. And even though it doesn't always work—even if it almost never works—it is still worthwhile. Even if the words are simply feathers in the wind, maybe they will delight a few people with their dance.

And somehow those words—even the ones that are feathers in the wind—they still have the ability to become bridges between me and you. I think that's important to remember. That your words, even the ones that are tossed into the wind, they are the bridges between you and everything else.

66

HAPPINESS IS AN IMAGINARY LINE IN THE SAND

I'VE WRITTEN ABOUT HOW THE NEW YEAR IS AN IMAGINARY LINE IN THE SAND. But of course, all lines are imaginary lines in the sand. From national borders to your property boundaries, we made them all up. And yet, countless wars and endless litigation have been waged over those imaginary lines.

Lately I've been reading little fragments of *The Untethered Soul* again. And that's got me considering the idea of unconditional happiness once more. The question the author poses is essentially, *Are you willing to be happy no matter what happens?*

It is a harder question to answer than you might think at first glance. I mean, pretty much everyone wants to be happy, right? The crux is, most of us don't really know what that means. What most people mean when they say they want to be happy is that they want everything in their lives to go the way they want. Pretty much everything. Pretty much all the time.

The problem with that is I don't know a single person whose life is like that. Now I think it is a fair observation to note that life is objectively easier for some people than it is for others. I'm thinking along the lines of Maslow's hierarchy of needs here. If you have no food and no place to get out of the weather, self-actualization is not your primary concern. But before we let the mind take us on that tangent, let's stick to the central tenet at issue.

We have equated getting what we want with happiness. But happiness and how the events of our lives play out are not at all the same thing. There are two problems with a definition of happiness that depends upon things going the way we want: (1) people who get everything they want are often the most miserable (think spoiled children or see my earlier thoughts on trust funders); and (2) there is generally no end to the things we want, and so the invisible line we must cross into happiness always stays several yards in front of us (consider billionaires who, despite having more money than 10 generations can spend, never stop chasing more and more money).

Under the common definition, people are willing to be happy so long as life meets their expectations for what they want. In other words, they want to be happy so long as everyone else in their lives acts exactly as they want them to at all times. Traffic is free-flowing, co-workers are congenial, boss is accommodating, paycheck is the right size, children are well-behaved, romantic partner is loving, kind, and supportive, their house, car and all electronic devices function properly, and everyone is healthy. All the time.

Does this sound reasonable? Of course not. And yet these are the conditions almost all of us have placed upon happiness. When we say we want to be happy, what we really mean is that we want absolutely everything in our lives to be easy. But that is not the same thing as happiness. And it is inevitably impossible to attain.

Happiness then must be something different from what we have imagined it to be. And coming to terms with that is the place where we must begin if we really want to be happy. We must break a lifetime of conditioning and begin to separate our life events from our quest for happiness. Otherwise, happiness is not possible. It is like having a wrapped present that you refuse to unwrap because it is so pretty. Our idea of happiness is so pretty, we refuse to take off the wrapping of our expectations, and so we will never to get to what is on the other side.

The most interesting thing I noticed about myself when I was considering this idea of unconditional happiness was the amount of resistance I immediately had to it. *I can't possibly be happy no mater what! That's too much to ask.* But I couldn't figure out what I was afraid of. Did I think agreeing to unconditional happiness somehow meant bad things would happen to me? Or maybe I thought it would invite bad things into my life just to test me. Or maybe my left-brain just couldn't find a box for this concept, because it is counter to a whole lifetime of coding.

I decided the resistance was either the mind short-circuiting because it is not wired for this kind of thinking or the ego raging against its diminishment in my life. Either way, committing to unconditional happiness feels way scarier than it should.

If one day you wake up and just decide to be happy, in spite of what your day has in store, how could there be a downside to that? You are going to experience bumps, obstacles, and roadblocks on your life path, no matter what. The only difference your decision to be happy makes is that these life experiences need not be frustrating, anger-inducing, or devastating. Your decision means only that you get to have peace of mind along the way. And yet, most of us will still resist the decision to be happy. Doesn't that seem crazy?

Yes, it seems crazy. But that doesn't change the reality of it, does it? So how do we mere mortals overcome our resistance to this idea? Here's where I get back to the beginning of this thread and the concept of imaginary lines.

When I read *The Untethered Soul* or Eckhart Tolle or any of the purveyors of this kind of life wisdom, I feel like I am looking at a picture of a beautiful mountain that I'll never be able to climb. Why is that? Why does my mind tell me that this may work for other people, but I will never be able to choose to be happy?

I think it's because unhappiness is like an addiction. And we are really reluctant to give up that next hit. Also, we are addicted to our ideas of ourselves and the world. The ideas about ourselves—our identities—are tied up in the ongoing story we tell ourselves all day. That story involves some measure of unhappiness. And so without unhappiness, who are we?

HAPPINESS IS AN IMAGINARY LINE IN THE SAND

Here's how happiness and a new year are the same. They are both imaginary lines in the sand. And they are both opportunities to experience life in a new way. But we have to be willing to hang up our old coats, so to speak, and put on something new. To reiterate Joseph Campbell's teaching, *We must be willing to let go of the life we planned so as to have the life that is waiting for us.*

Now, maybe that new way of life looks like jumping with both feet into a commitment to unconditional happiness. Or maybe it isn't that drastic. Maybe you give yourself some room to grow into that kind of thing. The point is you treat whatever decision you make as an invisible line in the sand. And you move forward. You buy yourself a fresh journal and begin to write a new story for yourself.

Is it an imaginary line? Sure. But only in the beginning. Once you begin to live this new story, something magic happens. It becomes real. And that feels like something even mere mortals like you and me can pull off.

BIBLIOGRAPHY

All of these essays made individual appearances elsewhere in the world before they came together to make this beautiful book.

1. "Each Day Asks This" *Reno Tahoe Tonight Magazine*, May 2013; *Rebelle Society*, July 17, 2013
2. "Begin" *Reno Tahoe Tonight Magazine*, Jan. 2014
3. "Where to Start" *Reno Tahoe Tonight Magazine*, Jan. 2016
4. "Start Over" *Reno Tahoe Tonight Magazine*, Jan. 2015
5. "Keep Finding Your Center" *Reno Tahoe Tonight Magazine*, April 2017
6. "Stay Curious" *Reno Tahoe Tonight Magazine*, Sept. 2015
7. "There Are Days" *Reno Tahoe Tonight Magazine*, Aug. 2013
8. "Grapple" *Reno Tahoe Tonight Magazine*, Oct. 2014
9. "Benefit of the Doubt" *Reno Tahoe Tonight Magazine*, Apr. 2013
10. "Finding Beauty in Darkness" *Reno Tahoe Tonight Magazine*, Nov. 2017
11. "The Unknowable World" *Reno Tahoe Tonight Magazine*, May 2017 (An Ocean of Dreams)
12. "Lessons From My Son" *Reno Tahoe Tonight Magazine*, June 2017
13. "Building the New World" *Reno Tahoe Tonight Magazine*, Aug. 2017
14. "Open" *Reno Tahoe Tonight Magazine*, May 2014

15. "Trust" *Reno Tahoe Tonight Magazine*, Mar. 2014
16. "Dig Deeper" *Reno Tahoe Tonight Magazine*, Feb. 2014
17. "The Hidden World" *Reno Tahoe Tonight Magazine*, June 2016
18. "How to Blend the Worlds" *Reno Tahoe Tonight Magazine*, Aug. 2016 (Blending the World)
19. "The Ingredients of Words" *Reno Tahoe Tonight Magazine*, Jan. 2012 (What's in a Word)
20. "Elevate the Word" *Reno Tahoe Tonight Magazine*, May 2016
21. "Let's Talk About Writing" *Reno Tahoe Tonight Magazine*, Sept. 2017
22. "You're Not the Boss of Me" *Reno Tahoe Tonight Magazine*, Aug. 2012
23. "Someday Words" *Reno Tahoe Tonight Magazine*, Dec. 2013
24. "Walking Lessons" *Alchemy of Words*, Nov. 8, 2019; *Medium*, Nov. 12, 2019
25. "Your Job is to Find Beauty" *Rebelle Society*, Oct. 29, 2013
26. "Save the World, Buy Art" *Reno Tahoe Tonight Magazine*, July 2015 (Buy Art)
27. "Believe in Art" *Reno Tahoe Tonight Magazine*, June 2013 (Good Grief)
28. "Storied Life" *Reno Tahoe Tonight Magazine*, Apr. 2012
29. "Notes on Madness & Art" *Alchemy of Words*
30. "Create It" *Reno Tahoe Tonight Magazine*, Nov. 2015
31. "Love" *Reno Tahoe Tonight Magazine*
32. "What is Love?" *Reno Tahoe Tonight Magazine*, Feb. 2016
33. "Lonely Hearts Club" *Reno Tahoe Tonight Magazine*, Feb. 2013

34. "The Heart of Ewe" *Reno Tahoe Tonight Magazine*, Apr. 2012
35. "WTAF" *Reno Tahoe Tonight Magazine*, Feb. 2017
36. "More Than This" *Reno Tahoe Tonight Magazine*, Sept. 2012
37. "You Belong Here" *Reno Tahoe Tonight Magazine*, Apr. 2016
38. "Give It Up" *Reno Tahoe Tonight Magazine*, Sept. 2016
39. "We're All Outsiders" *Reno Tahoe Tonight Magazine*, Nov. 2016
40. "The Things We Want" *Reno Tahoe Tonight Magazine*, Oct. 2016 (Follow Your Craving)
41. "Follow Me" *Reno Tahoe Tonight Magazine*, Oct. 2015
42. "Howl" *Reno Tahoe Tonight Magazine*, July 2014
43. "A Space Between the Notes" *Alchemy of Words, Medium*, Mar. 18, 2020
44. "Roiling In Dough" *Reno Tahoe Tonight Magazine*, Mar. 2015 (Roll Out the Dough)
45. "Be Free" *Alchemy of Words,* Jan. 23, 2020; *Medium* Feb. 4, 2020
46. "A Void Is Not Something You Fill" *Reno Tahoe Tonight Magazine*, Oct. 2017 (You Cannot Fill the Void)
47. "Enough" *Reno Tahoe Tonight Magazine*, Nov. 2013
48. "How to Navigate an Inversion" *Alchemy of Words*, May 30, 2020; *Medium* June 7, 2020
49. "Fight Back" *Reno Tahoe Tonight Magazine*, Mar. 2015
50. "Go Ahead" *Reno Tahoe Tonight Magazine*, Apr. 2015
51. "Be Brave" *Reno Tahoe Tonight Magazine*, Aug. 2015
52. "Unravel" *Reno Tahoe Tonight Magazine*, June 2014
53. "Be That" *Reno Tahoe Tonight Magazine*, Dec. 2015
54. "Thrive" *Reno Tahoe Tonight Magazine*, Aug 2014

55. "Feelings Are Like Cats" *Medium*, May 18, 2018 (How to Feel Alive Again)
56. "Be Kind" *Reno Tahoe Tonight Magazine*, June 2015
57. "Lighten Up" *Reno Tahoe Tonight Magazine*, Dec. 2012
58. "What Are You Laughing At?" *Reno Tahoe Tonight Magazine*, Nov. 2012
59. "The Shifting World" *Reno Tahoe Tonight Magazine*, July 2013
60. "Don't Stop" *Rebelle Society*, June 28, 2013; *Alchemy of Words*, July 18, 2013
61. "Splintered Oneness" *Reno Tahoe Tonight Magazine* March 2016 (Going to Write)
62. "Life Would Like Your Full Attention" *Reno Tahoe Tonight Magazine*, Nov. 2014 (Look)
63. "The Art of Holding Hands" *Reno Tahoe Tonight Magazine*, Oct. 2018
64. "The Earth is an Enlightened Master" *Alchemy of Words*, June 18, 2020 (The Sentient Earth); *Medium*, June 26, 2020
65. "Feather in the Wind" *Reno Tahoe Tonight Magazine*, Dec. 2017
66. "Happiness is An Imaginary Line in the Sand" *Medium* Jan. 9, 2020

ACKNOWLEDGMENTS

This book is in your hands because of the efforts of many people. Though it is not possible to list all those who had a hand in this compilation, I will endeavor to name a few who stand out. First in line is Oliver X, because he held space in his magazine month after month for me and the words I strung together, for more than six years. From there we follow a thread that starts with an essay I read in the online forum Rebelle Society, which inspired me to submit my writing to them. Andrea Balt and Tanya Markell picked up the thread when they welcomed me into their Rebelle tribe and featured my work. Next comes Jeanette LeBlanc, who continued to weave this thread into her Wild Heart circle of writers, who became my friend in the process, and who is the author of the Rebelle Society piece that first inspired me, *Blessed Be Your Longing*.

When I had carried this thread through enough essays, it was Lorna Benedict who suggested they might belong together, all in one place, where more people could read them. Lorna also read the early drafts and provided feedback and support, as did my my dear friend and reliable cheerleader Ana Bobadilla. Along the road to collecting enough writings to fill a book, I received valuable advice and other generosities from Cindy Geddes, M.T. Cain, Justin Power, and Randy Davila. Picking back up the thread from earlier, Jeannette LeBlanc introduced me to Jacob Nordby, who, among other things, invited me to

Santa Fe, where I walked on fire and changed my life. The Santa Fe thread then leads to Lisa McCourt and Mellissae Lucia, who I owe special thanks for their advance review of this work and for their extraordinary support and encouragement. With the help of each of these people and many who are unnamed, and the wisdom they've stitched into the fabric of me, I had the audacity to present these essays to Homebound Publications, who gratefully agreed to publish them.

Through all this, Lynell Garfield protected my writing solitude, made sure our child was fed, and reminded me to schedule semi-regular date nights. August was no help with the actual writing, but he continues to provide me with endless material. And then we come to you, the readers, who not only complete the work of art, but pick up the threads and continue the weaving.

ABOUT THE AUTHOR

Thomas Lloyd Qualls is a writer, a condition that is apparently incurable. He is also a storyteller, the former owner of a music festival, a licensed attorney who has overturned two death sentences, and a one-time vagabond who used to wander the globe with a backpack and three changes of clothes.

What he means to say is that he is a human being who, so far, has done all these things. He'll probably do more things not on this list.

With all of his creative work, he seeks to bridge the worlds of literary and spiritual and to blur the lines between what is real and what is imagined. He also strives to create worlds where labels are difficult to affix. He loves Pablo Neruda's poem *Too Many Names*.

Thomas lives in the high desert beauty of Northern Nevada, along with the children's author Lynell Garfield and their son. You can follow his trail of words and other misadventures at www.tlqonline.com.

BASED IN THE BERKSHIRE MOUNTAINS, MASS.

At Wayfarer Books we believe poetry is the language of the earth. We believe words—shaped like rivers through wild places—can change the shape of the world. We publish poets and writers and renegades who stand outside of mainstream culture—poets, essayists, and storytellers whose work might withstand the scrutiny of crows and coyotes, those who are cryptic and floral, the crepuscular, and the queer-at-heart. We are more than just a publisher but a community of writers. Our mission is to produce books that can serve as a compass and map to all wayfarers through wild terrain.

WAYFARERBOOKS.ORG

www.ingramcontent.com/pod-product-compliance
Lightning Source LLC
LaVergne TN
LVHW091711070526
838199LV00050B/2357